W9-DIM-028

FLORIDA STATE
UNIVERSITY LIBRARIES

AUG 10 1995

Tallahassee, Florida

Contemporary Challenges:
American Business
in a Global Economy

THE JOSEPH I. LUBIN MEMORIAL LECTURES
NUMBER 7

Edited by
Daniel E. Diamond

Contemporary Challenges: American Business in a Global Economy

The Joseph I. Lubin Memorial Lectures, 1992–1994

The Joseph I. Lubin Memorial Lectures
New York University
Leonard N. Stern School of Business

NEW YORK UNIVERSITY PRESS

NEW YORK AND LONDON

HE
8815
C658
1995

NEW YORK UNIVERSITY PRESS
New York and London

Copyright © 1995 by New York University

Library of Congress Cataloging-in-Publication Data
Contemporary challenges : American business in a global economy /
edited by Daniel E. Diamond.
p. cm.—(The Joseph I. Lubin memorial lectures ; no. 7)
"Lectures presented at New York University's Stern School of
Business in 1992, 1993, and 1994"—Pref.
ISBN 0-8147-1868-X
1. Television broadcasting—United States. 2. Television
broadcasting. 3. Telecommunication. 4. United States—Economic
policy—1981– 5. Competition, International. I. Diamond, Daniel
E., 1929– . II. Series.
HE8815.C658   1995
384—dc20   94-44880
                CIP

New York University Press books are printed on acid-free paper,
and their binding materials are chosen for strength and durability.

Manufactured in the United States of America

10   9   8   7   6   5   4   3   2   1

This volume is dedicated with thanks and appreciation from Barbara Lubin Goldsmith to Daniel E. Diamond upon his retirement as Vice Dean of New York University's Stern School of Business and Dean of the School's Undergraduate College, 1985–1995. He will continue to serve the School and the University as a valued member of the faculty.

—Dean George G. Daly
Stern School of Business

CONTENTS

PREFACE

Daniel E. Diamond

Dean, the Undergraduate College
New York University
Leonard N. Stern School of Business

The Joseph I. Lubin Memorial Lectures were established and funded in perpetuity through the generosity of the late Joseph I. Lubin, a distinguished business, philanthropic, and civic leader. Mr. Lubin wished to provide a public forum for the discussion and practical application of economic and management principles and theories.

Mr. Lubin, a graduate of Pace College and New York University's School of Law, was a cofounder and senior partner of the nationally known accounting firm Eisner and Lubin. A CPA, he was a major contributor to the accounting profession serving as chairman of the New York State Board of Certified Public Accountant Examiners, vice president of the New York State Society of Certified Public Accountants, and a member of the Council of the American

Institute of Certified Public Accountants. He was also active in other business areas, including serving as chairman of the board of the United Cigar–Whelan Store Corporation, the Pepsi-Cola Company, and the Phoenix Securities Corporation. In addition to other real estate holdings, in the late 1950s he purchased the Astor Hotel on Times Square. As a grade school student, he had worked at the hotel as a page boy.

Mr. Lubin's humanism and beneficent impact on our society was evidenced by his many interests and generous contributions. In particular, institutions of higher learning benefited from Mr. Lubin's largess. At New York University, in addition to establishing the Lubin Memorial Lectures at the Leonard N. Stern School of Business, he, together with the estate of his partner, Joseph Eisner, financed the Eisner and Lubin Auditorium at the University's Loeb Student Center. He made a major contribution to Pace University, which named its School of Business and Administration in his honor. In addition, he made sizable donations to the Hebrew University of Jerusalem, Syracuse University, and Yeshiva University's Albert Einstein College of Medicine.

Joseph I. Lubin served as a trustee of New York

University and Pace College, as well as being an
overseer at the Albert Einstein College of Medicine.
In recognition of his generous benefaction and
involvement, Mr. Lubin received honorary doctor-
ates from Yeshiva University, Syracuse University,
Pace University, and New York Law School. Moreover, Mr. Lubin served as a director of the Henry
Street Settlement; Children's Village in Dobbs
Ferry, New York; the New Rochelle Hospital; and
the Union of American Hebrew Congregations. For
some fifteen years, he was national treasurer of the
United Jewish Appeal and the Joint Distribution
Committee.

This book contains the Lubin Memorial Lectures
presented at New York University's Stern School of
Business in 1992, 1993, and 1994. They were,
respectively, ninth, tenth, and eleventh in the series. The previous lectures were:

1983   The World Banking System in a Context
of Crisis
Andrew F. Brimmer, President of Brimmer
Company, Inc., and Chairman of the
Monetary Policy Forum
Utah Senator Jake Garn, Chairman of the
Senate Banking Committee

John J. Creedon, Chairman of the Executive
Committee of the Board of Directors,
Metropolitan Life Insurance Company

1991   Keeping America's Options Open: The Key
to Future Energy Abundance
Allen E. Murray, Chairman and Chief Executive Officer, Mobil Corporation

The Lubin Memorial Lectures are made possible by
the Joseph I. Lubin Fund and this book by Mr.
Lubin's daughter, Barbara Goldsmith.

INTERNATIONAL TELECOMMUNICATIONS: ITS GROWTH AND SIGNIFICANCE TO THE WORLD

Michael Jay Solomon

President, Warner Bros. International Television Distribution

*Remarks by Michael Jay Solomon
on the occasion of the annual
Joseph I. Lubin Memorial Lecture
10 March 1992*

*New York University
Leonard N. Stern School of Business*

My lecture covers the international television market, but in order to understand the full picture, it is important to review the early days of U.S. television.

Commercial television was launched in 1939, but it wasn't until after World War II, in 1946, that TV became the "primary message." In 1946, there were just 6,000 television sets in use. One year later, there were 142,000. Four years later, 9.7 million homes had TV sets. By 1952, less than six years later, the number had more than doubled to 21.8 million sets. In 1991, the U.S. had 91.5 million television households, many with two or more televisions.

Today, we are seeing this remarkable growth in foreign markets. Television has had enormous effects on world societies. Take, for instance, Tiananmen Square, the Gulf War, the fall of the Berlin Wall, freedom in Eastern Europe, and the failed coup in Russia.

Television as a "primary message" has been partially responsible for the break-up of communism. News and information programs are the most important programs in the world and have led to many closed societies opening their lines of communication by stunting governmental efforts at news censorship.

The emergence of these new "democratic" societies has allowed American companies to import product into countries that are starved for entertainment programming. In early 1992, we launched a

THE GLOBAL TELEVISION MARKET

	WORLD	U.S.	%
MARKETS	178	1	
POPULATION	5.3b	250m	4.7%
TV'S	906m	184m	20%
AD EXPENDITURE $	64.1b	29.1b	46%

SOURCE: CARAT, 1991

"Warner Week" in Russia, and the response was overwhelming.

We can see that C.I.S., Eastern Europe, India and China will want more programming, as they begin to watch U.S. product. New stations have been licensed throughout Europe, and the demand for U.S. product continues to increase.

The television business has dramatically changed over the past ten years. The United States is no longer the exclusive player in the TV production

> **GROWTH OF INTERNATIONAL TELEVISION**
>
> **1980's**
> EUROPEAN TELEVISION
>
> **1990'S**
> ASIAN TELEVISION

and distribution business, although it dominates 46 percent of the world's advertising expenditure, with under 25 percent of the overall population.

The 1980s were a time of growth in the European marketplace, and the 1990s will see the growth of television in Asia.

Let's look at the growth of television in Europe.

EUROPEAN TELEVISION GROWTH		
STATISTICS	1980	1990
# TV STATIONS	29	119 +
AD INVESTMENT	N/A	+297% ($65b)
AD SHARE FOR TV (FROM ALL OTHER MEDIA)	17.5%	30.3%
AD MINUTES P/WEEK	N/A	25,000

SOURCE: ASSOCIATION OF COMMERCIAL T.V.

TERRESTRIAL NETWORK CHANNELS		
	1980	1990
U.K.	3	5
GERMANY	3	8
FRANCE	3	6
SPAIN	2	5+REGIONALS
ITALY	4	8
NETHERLANDS	2	4

SOURCE: CARAT, 1991

Most television was government controlled in the 1970s. In the 1980s governments began to issue commercial broadcasting licenses. In 1980, there were 29 television stations within the 12 E.C. countries, and today there are over 119.

If we look at this expansion on a country by

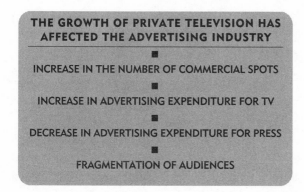

THE GROWTH OF PRIVATE TELEVISION HAS
AFFECTED THE ADVERTISING INDUSTRY

■

INCREASE IN THE NUMBER OF COMMERCIAL SPOTS

■

INCREASE IN ADVERTISING EXPENDITURE FOR TV

■

DECREASE IN ADVERTISING EXPENDITURE FOR PRESS

■

FRAGMENTATION OF AUDIENCES

country level, we see that most markets have doubled the number of channels, with Italy, Germany, and Spain leading the expansion.

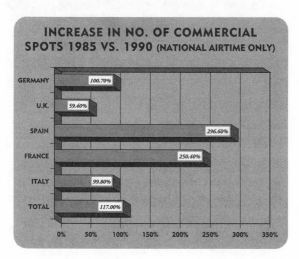

INCREASE IN NO. OF COMMERCIAL
SPOTS 1985 VS. 1990 (NATIONAL AIRTIME ONLY)

GERMANY	100.70%
U.K.	59.40%
SPAIN	296.60%
FRANCE	250.40%
ITALY	99.80%
TOTAL	117.00%

0% 50% 100% 150% 200% 250% 300% 350%

9

Note: 98 percent of Europe's adult population reads newspapers.

The increase in commercial broadcasters has resulted in an increase in the number of available television advertising spots.

The increase in television advertising has resulted in a decrease in advertising for newspapers and magazines. While the advertising share for television has increased by 13 percent, newspaper and magazine advertising has dropped 13 percent over a ten-year period.

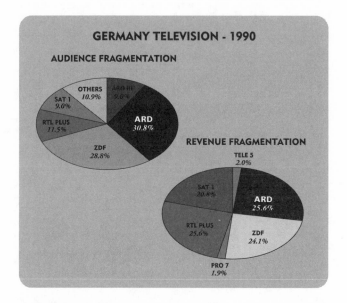

The additional private stations have resulted in audience fragmentation and advertising revenue fragmentation. Aggressive commercial stations have been able to successfully attract advertisers, although they may not represent the majority of the audience.

The advertising revenue fragmentation is a result of government restrictions that are placed on public broadcasters. These differences will be addressed later in my presentation.

In the 1980s, the expansion in European televi-

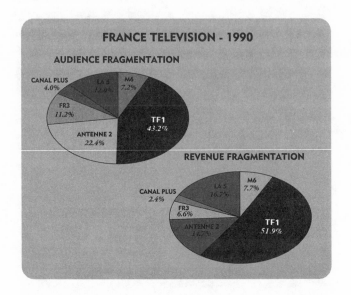

FRANCE TELEVISION - 1990

AUDIENCE FRAGMENTATION

- CANAL PLUS 4.0%
- LA 5 12.0%
- M6 7.2%
- FR3 11.2%
- ANTENNE 2 22.4%
- TF1 43.2%

REVENUE FRAGMENTATION

- CANAL PLUS 2.4%
- LA 5 16.7%
- M6 7.7%
- FR3 6.6%
- ANTENNE 2 14.7%
- TF1 51.9%

sion was in terrestrial broadcasting. In Asia, the new private stations are direct broadcast satellite. With this technology, which has the capability for multi-channel signals, we predict that the Asian market will develop at a faster pace in the 90s than Europe did in the 80s.

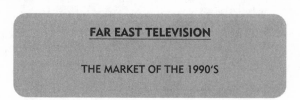

FAR EAST TELEVISION

THE MARKET OF THE 1990'S

SATELLITE TELEVISION		
AUSTRALIA	1993-4	17.5M
INDONESIA	1988	187.7M
JAPAN	1991	123.6M
KOREA	1992	45.2M
MALAYSIA	1988 &1992	18.3M
NEW ZEALAND	1989	3.5M
SINGAPORE	1992	2.8M
TAIWAN	1992	20.5
THAILAND	1988 & 1991	58.8M
SRI LANKA	1990	17.5M

It is predicted that at least five new satellite services will be launched in the Far East in Malaysia, Singapore, Korea, Taiwan and Australia. (Note: current satellites are relaying free-TV signals. We are encouraging encryption. This will lead to pay-TV.) The quick expansion of local satellite technology is a direct result of pan-Asian satellites like Hutchvision, which have enormous footprints throughout the Far East. Hutchvision emanates from Hong Kong, but is receivable in all of Southeast Asia.

The invasion of these foreign signals has threat-

PAN ASIAN TELEVISION PROGRAMMING

HUTCHVISION
PRIME SPORTS
MANDARIN CHINESE CHANNEL
BBC NEWS CHANNEL
STAR TV ENTERTAINMENT CHANNEL

CNN

ESPN

HBO
COMING SOON

ened many of the local governments, especially Indonesia and Malaysia, where the governments are Muslim. One of the best examples of this cultural invasion took place during the Gulf War. Malaysian and Indonesian citizens were able to watch CNN on satellite, but prior to this all available news was censored by the local government.

Let's examine the Japanese television market, since it is the most sophisticated in the Far East. Japanese television has four public channels (two on direct broadcast satellite) and five commercial networks. They also have two new pay and one cable network. Private commercial stations origi-

JAPANESE TELEVISION

STATION	TYPE OF STATION	SIGNAL	YEAR ORIGIN
NHK GENERAL	NON COMMERCIAL	TERRESTRIAL	1950
NHK EDUCATIONAL	NON COMMERCIAL	TERRESTRIAL	1950
NHK DBS1	NON COMMERCIAL	DBS	1988
NHK DBS2	NON COMMERCIAL	DBS	1988
TBS	COMMERCIAL	TERRESTRIAL	1955
NTV	COMMERCIAL	TERRESTRIAL	1953
TV ASHAI	COMMERCIAL	TERRESTRIAL	1959
FUJI TV	COMMERCIAL	TERRESTRIAL	1959
TV TOKYO	COMMERCIAL	TERRESTRIAL	1964
JSB	PAY	DBS	1991
STAR CHANNEL	PAY	CABLE	1989
SUPER CHANNEL	BASIC	CABLE	1989

nated over 30 years ago, and today the Japanese broadcasters are expanding and enriching their market through pay TV and direct broadcast satellite.

Note: U.S. commercial TV since 1939 (NBC-1939) (ABC-1948) (CBS-1941)

The Japanese commercial broadcasters have long since competed for their potential audience and have battled for their share of advertising revenue.

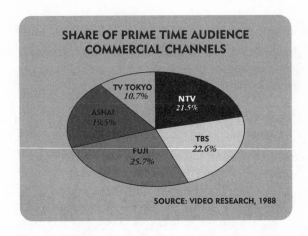

There has been no dramatic change in Japanese commercial broadcasting in the past ten years.

In Europe, many of the broadcasters were unable to successfully predict fragmentation, since there was no European prototype for comparison.

As a sophisticated and culturally distinct market, with a long history of commercial broadcasting, Japan has concentrated on developing their local production industry. This has allowed them to produce product with distinctly Japanese themes for local cultural taste.

There are no program import quotas in Japan, and yet American programming shares average less than 5 percent on commercial networks.

ANNUAL FOREIGN PROGRAMMING JAPANESE COMMERCIAL NETWORKS		
STATION	#HOURS	%STATION'S TELECASTING
NTV	284	3.4%
TBS	395	4.6%
FUJI TV	386	4.5%
TV ASHAI	285	3.5%
TV TOKYO	788	9.4%
		SOURCE: MPEAA, 1991

We can see a pattern in the evolution of private television.

Japan, a highly developed commercial market, has concentrated on building a strong local production industry. Europe is beginning to develop a strong local production industry, and is reducing its acquisition of imported product. Asia's birth in private television and direct broadcast satellite will result in an increase in import product. Eastern Europe and other underdeveloped commercial markets will make progress towards developing private television.

Each country has its own legislation regarding broadcasting and advertising.

There are two systems of broadcasting in Europe

COUNTRY	MARKET SOPHISTICATION
JAPAN	HIGHLY DEVELOPED COMMERCIAL MARKET
EUROPE	DEVELOPED COMMERCIAL MARKET
ASIA	EMERGING COMMERCIAL MARKET
EASTERN EUROPE	UNDEVELOPED COMMERCIAL MARKET

and they are referred to as private and public broadcasting. Public broadcasters are usually government controlled and financed through taxes and fees. Private broadcasters are privately owned and financed through advertising.

**PRIVATE
VS.
PUBLIC BROADCASTING**

If we examine broadcast advertising restrictions for public broadcasters, we can see that each country formulates its own conclusions with regard to television advertising.

In England, the BBC is restricted from any form of advertising. Their budget is collected via fees/taxes charged to each household. At a fee of £70 per household multiplied by 20 million households, the BBC budget averages approximately $2.3 billion U.S. dollars annually.

In Germany, ARD & ZDF are restricted to 20 minutes of advertising a day prior to 8:00 p.m. There is no advertising on Sundays or holidays. They are also financed through fees which average DM24 per month, per household X 24 million households averaging $3.4 billion dollars (U.S.) annually.

Italy and France are limited to approximately 7 minutes advertising per hour. Spain public TV receives no government tax money and functions as a private broadcaster, competing with other private Spanish networks for advertising revenue.

The private sector is not under the same restrictions reserved for the public sector. Even in those

PUBLIC BROADCASTERS		
COUNTRY	STATION	ADVERTISING
ENGLAND	BBC	NONE
GERMANY	ARD	LIMITED
	ZDF	LIMITED
ITALY	RAI	LIMITED
FRANCE	ANTENNE 2	LIMITED
	FR-3	LIMITED
SPAIN	RTVE	UNLIMITED

PRIVATE BROADCASTERS

COUNTRY	STATION	ADVERTISING
ENGLAND	ITV	UNLIMITED
	CH4	UNLIMITED
	BSKYB	UNLIMITED
GERMANY	RTL+	UNLIMITED
	PRO7	UNLIMITED
	TELE 5	UNLIMITED
ITALY	RETE-4	LIMITED
	ITALIA-1	LIMITED
	CANALE-5	LIMITED
FRANCE	TF1	LIMITED
	LA CINQ	LIMITED
	M6	LIMITED
SPAIN	ANTENA 3	UNLIMITED
	TELE 5	UNLIMITED
	REGIONALS	UNLIMITED

territories, such as Italy, the commercial stations are allowed 12 minutes of advertising time per hour as opposed to the 7 minutes that the public broadcasters are allowed.

In England, Germany and Spain, the private stations have no commercial restrictions.

The private stations receive no government taxes or financial assistance. For many, advertising is the sole source of revenue.

We have seen that government regulations distort the relationship between economics and broadcast advertising. The governments regulate three major

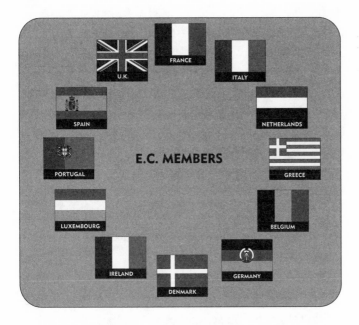

areas of broadcasting: 1) number of channels, 2) advertising prices, 3) airtime.

But there is another distortion, which is based on "protectionism" called quotas. Governments restrict the amount of imported product which a station may acquire and demand that stations primarily broadcast local origin or E.C. product. It is important to note that there are no import quotas in Germany and they have a very strong local production industry.

BROADCAST QUOTAS / EUROPE	
FRANCE	AT LEAST 40% MUST BE OF FRENCH ORIGIN
	AT LEAST 10% MUST BE OF EC ORIGIN
	40% MAY BE NOT OF NON-EC ORIGIN
ITALY	40% FEATURE FILMS MUST BE ITALIAN & EC
	IN 1994 QUOTA RISES TO 51%
PORTUGAL	40% OF TOTAL PROGRAMMING MUST BE IN PORTUGUESE
	30% OF THE 40% MUST BE PORTUGUESE ORIGIN
SPAIN	40% OF PROGRAMMING ON COMMERCIAL TV MUST
	BE OF EC ORIGIN
	40% OF FILMS MUST BE OF EC ORIGIN
	50% OF FILMS MUST BE IN SPANISH LANGUAGE
	NOT DUBBED
	NO QUOTA FOR PUBLIC TELEVISION
U.K.	86% OF BROADCAST TIME MUST BE EC/BRITISH ORIGIN
	JANUARY, 1993, NON-EC/BRITISH ORIGIN FOR
	COMMERCIAL TV WILL RISE TO 35%

Even without the quota systems, U.S. product accounts for a very small share of the overall world-wide transmission schedule.

In a courageous but futile attempt, the E.C. directive was created to standardize broadcasting and advertising restrictions across Europe. The E.C. decided to allow TV channels to broadcast across frontier barriers, based on the notion of Europe now being "one market." In multilingual countries (like Belgium and Switzerland), this will hinder the small stations in their programming endeavors. Advertisers will have to pay for this additional audience,

1990
LOCAL VS. U.S. PROGRAMMING
TRANSMISSION TIME PROVIDED

TERRITORY	LOCAL ORIGIN	U.S.
AFRICA	85%	10%
ASIA/PACIFIC	77%	19%
CANADA	73%	27%
CARIBBEAN	43%	54%
CENTRAL/S. AMERICA	63%	33%
EASTERN EUROPE	93%	1%
MIDDLE EAST	75%	13%
REST EUROPE	79%	13%
U.S.	89%	89%

SOURCE: SCREEN DIGEST/INTERMEDIA

even though their product may not be available in that country.

The E.C. directive included restrictions on advertisement content, one of the new laws being "ads may not promote activities detrimental to the environment." The E.C. banned an ad for a battery saw, which went something like this:

A man in the forest is cutting down trees with his battery saw. The battery dies, and the man throws it behind his back, retrieves a new battery which he replaces in the saw, and continues to cut down trees. The E.C. did not ban the ad because the man had cut down trees, they banned it because he threw the battery away in the forest!

E.C. DIRECTIVE
CROSS FRONTIER BROADCASTING

ONLY COVERS TELEVISION

BANS ADVERTISING FOR TOBACCO & PRESCRIPTION MEDICINE

LIMITS COMMERCIAL AIRTIME TO 15% DAILY TRANSMISSION

SETS GUIDELINES FOR:
ADS FOR CHILDREN AND PROGRAM SPONSORSHIP'

ALLOWS TV CHANNELS TO CROSS FRONTIERS IN THE E.C.

The European convention of 1989 reviewed the E.C. directive and suggested modifications for many of the stringent rules that the E.C. had placed on the broadcasters. The European Convention confirmed the notion that it is close to impossible to initiate across-the-board legislation, based on the enormous cultural and linguistic differences in Europe.

This brings us to the story of the E.C.'s attitudes towards carrots:

The E.C. reviewed quality standards for the export of foods and decided that jam must be made of 90 percent fruit. Portugal, one of the members of the E.C., objected to this since their number one jam was made with carrots. After many months

EUROPEAN CONVENTION 1989
TRANSFRONTIER TELEVISION

SIMILAR GUIDELINES ON ADVERTISING AS THE E.C. DIRECTIVE - BUT ALLOWS PIPE TOBACCO/CIGAR ADVERTISING

ARTICLE 16 ENABLES COUNTRIES TO BLOCK ADS DIRECTED AT AUDIENCES IN THAT COUNTRY IF THE ADVERTISEMENTS CIRCUMVENT NAT'L LAWS

ARTICLE 24 ALLOWS A COUNTRY TO SUSPEND A BROADCAST TRANSMISSION UPLINK FOR 8 MONTHS

ALLOWS COUNTRIES TO BLOCK TELEVISION CHANNELS FROM OTHER COUNTRIES

of deliberations, the E.C. finally announced that from this day forward in Europe, "the carrot was a fruit"!

The future markets are those which have a large untapped population with the potential for economic growth. We perceive these areas as growing television markets and believe that India, Eastern Europe, and C.I.S. have the most future potential of the new markets.

India's TV is dominated by the state-run broadcaster Doordarsham, founded in 1959. The network's import product accounts for only 5 percent of its schedule and is usually restricted to one half-hour program and one feature film each month. Doordarsham faces increased competition from Asian satellites and cable. The Indian government has tried to create a national cable and satellite monitoring service to handle foreign signals. They are also evaluating the potential of granting new television licenses to private broadcasters. With a population of 833.4 million people and a government who is reevaluating the broadcast industry, U.S. distributors have a potential to tap one of the largest populations in the world.

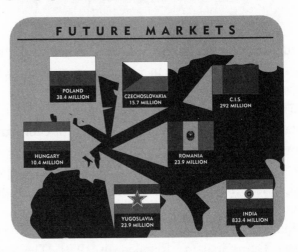

FUTURE MARKETS

POLAND
38.4 MILLION

CZECHOSLOVAKIA
15.7 MILLION

C.I.S.
292 MILLION

HUNGARY
10.4 MILLION

ROMANIA
23.9 MILLION

YUGOSLAVIA
23.9 MILLION

INDIA
833.4 MILLION

The Commonwealth of Independent States is in a state of flux. The failed coup in August of 1989 has been followed by a rapid disintegration of the old order, with most of the republics declaring independence.

Even with the frail economic environment and fledgling democracies, Eastern Europe has the potential for economic growth. Cable television is a growing force in these markets, funded mostly by outside investors like HBO in Hungary. There is minimal local product, as the Eastern European countries were importing communist programs from the U.S.S.R. Now that there is a breakdown in communism, broadcasters must find other sources for programming.

THE DISTRIBUTION BUSINESS
A) WHY WE SELL
B) HOW WE SELL
C) FUTURE DEVELOPMENT
D) WHY BROADCASTERS BUY U.S. PRODUCT

Most network series are produced with a deficit. This means that the network license fee does not cover the production expenses. The deficit is primarily recouped in international sales, and as production costs have risen, international television has played a more significant role. The average one-hour series costs $1.2 million per episode to produce, and the networks pay an average of $900,000, leaving a deficit of $300,000.

The chart below identifies the deficit financing on a Warner Bros. series only. *Knots Landing,* in its eleventh year, is the only one-hour series produced without a deficit.

If we were to calculate the Warner Bros. one-hour deficit position for the 1991–92 season it would add up to the following numbers:

Average deficit = $300,000

Average number of episodes per season = 22

$300,000 × 22 = $6.6 million

Six series with a deficit of $6.6 million = $39.6 million for one season.

In addition to the current on air product, we are also continually responsible for reducing the deficit on one hour series that have been canceled, i.e. *China Beach* and *Midnight Caller.*

Comedies are also produced at a deficit. Most comedies average $650,000 per episode in production costs and $200,000 in deficit financing. Comedies are able to recoup their deficit when and if the show lasts four years on a network. When the show has enough episodes, it is then syndicated throughout the U.S., which means it is sold on a market by

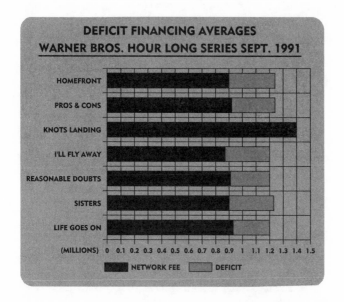

market basis as a Monday through Friday stripped program. A syndicated comedy can make between $600K–700K per half hour in its first cycle of syndication.

Feature films are the number one product type in the international markets, with the exception of some very successful series, like *The Bold and The Beautiful* in Italy.

When we sell series, we sell by production year, which averages 22 episodes for full season shows and 13 for midseason shows. As soon as a network

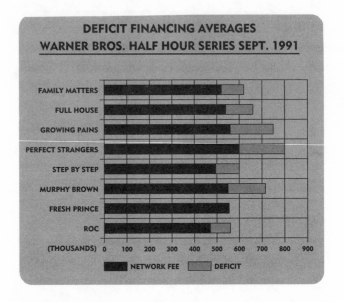

places an order for a series, we are selling it to the international broadcasters.

The growth in European broadcasting has created a competitive market which results in two scenarios:

- Local territory hits can be canceled in the U.S. after only 13 or 22 episodes (Examples, *Flash* and *Max Headroom,* which were very popular overseas and not in the U.S.).

• Broadcasters commit to a full season of a series and it does not perform well in their local market.

These are the risks associated with TV program sales and acquisitions.

HOW WE SELL

A) FEATURE FILMS LEAD PACKAGES
   (MOST OF THE TIME)
B) SERIES SOLD BY PRODUCTION YEAR
C) COMPETITIVE MARKET RISKS

The changes in the broadcasting community will lead to changes in sales methods and support. We are pursuing two areas for the future: promotion and research.

Broadcasters are becoming more sophisticated in their buying strategies and we are supplying additional data, including U.S. ratings, popularity scores, international ratings, on-air promos, and international rating success stories.

In the future, we will need to produce personalized on-air promos (example: Candice Bergen saying watch me on a French network). We will need to design specific target demographic promotional campaigns for the foreign market.

> **FUTURE DEVELOPMENTS**
>
> A NEW SALES APPROACH
> A) LEARNING TO DIFFERENTIATE OUR PRODUCT
> B) ASSISTING BROADCASTERS IN PROMOTING PRODUCT
> C) USE OF INTERNATIONAL RATINGS

The U.S. series do not perform as well as local origin series in the foreign market.

In 1991, the top U.S. series in France ranked #40 out of all programs broadcast in a month, and usually averaged a 14.5 rating. The same holds true for Italy and the U.K.:

U.K. top US series = Rank #30 Baywatch

Italy Top US = Rank #61 Bold & Beautiful

Average Rating 13.2

As well as . . .

Germany Top US series = Rank #66 Matlock

Average rating 15.0

TOP SERIES OF 1990

	FRANCE	RTG	ITALY	RTG	U.K.	RTG
1	NAVARRO	23.2	UNBAMBINO IN FUGA	18.0	CORONATION STREET	43.9
2	L'ADDITION EST POUR MOI	20.0	PRONTO SOCCORSO	15.0	EASTENDERS	43.9
3	DOSSIERS L'INSPECTEUR LAV.	18.2	DONNA D'ONORE	14.2	NEIGHBORS	40.0
4	IMOGENE	17.6	ILVIGILE URBANO	14.0	INSPECTOR MORSE	30.5
5	LES CINQ DENIERES MINUTES	17.4	BOLD & BEAUTIFUL	13.7	HOME & AWAY	29.0

Spain is the exception. Many of their series are imported from Latin America and the U.S.

TOP SERIES OF 1990

	GERMANY	RTG	SPAIN	RTG
1	DIESE DROMBUSHS	36.7	BRIGIDA CENTRAL	32.7
2	HOTEL PARADIES	34.1	CRISTAL	29.3
3	DERRICK	32.2	LA MUJER DE TU VIDA	29.2
4	TATORT	31.1	GOLDEN GIRLS	27.9
5	EIN FALL FUR ZWEI	28.7	FALCON CREST	26.6

Production and distribution companies have always tried to seek a product's full potential. For us, this means exploiting the product in as many different mediums as possible. Using Batman as an example, the character was part of our D.C. Comics library and was selected as the star character for a feature film. Once the feature film was produced, it was released in theaters and then cross-promoted and released as merchandising, a soundtrack, publishing, homevideo, pay per view and so on. . . . As new mediums are developed, like pay per view,

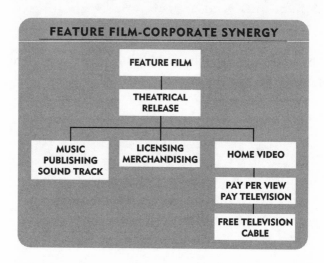

we will create a window or amount of time of exclusive exploitation for the new medium.

U.S. feature films are the highest rated genre import. In the U.K., all of the top five features for 1990 were U.S. The British consider the James Bond movies local origin, but they are distributed by United Artists, a U.S. company.

TOP RATED FEATURES FOR 1990 U.K.					
TITLE	STN.	RTG.	#VIEWERS	ORIGIN	RELEASE YEAR
E.T.	BBC1	33.6	17,478,048	U.S.	1982
VIEW TO A KILL	ITV	32.5	16,905,850	U.S./U.K.	1985
OCTOPUSSY	ITV	30.5	15,865,490	U.S./U.K.	1983
FOR YOUR EYES ONLY	ITV	29.2	15,189,256	U.S./U.K.	1981
WILD CATS	ITV	25.0	13,004,500	U.S.	1986

SOURCE: EURODIENCE/BARB

In Italy three out of the top five features were of U.S. origin.

TOP RATED FEATURES FOR 1990 ITALY					
TITLE	STN.	RTG.	#VIEWERS	ORIGIN	RELEASE YEAR
O E MIA SORELLA	RAI1	23.1	12,759,978	ITALY	1987
IL PICCOLO DIAVOLO	CAN5	20.3	11,213,314	ITALY	1988
COBRA	CAN5	17.1	9,445,698	U.S.	1986
ROCKY IV	CAN 5	16.8	9,279,984	U.S.	1985
SHOOT TO KILL	RAI1	16.2	8,948,556	U.S.	1987

SOURCE: EURODIENCE/STUDIO FRASI

The same holds true for Spain. With the exception of news and sports, theatrical films are the most consistent rating winners.

Following the example used on feature film synergy, many companies are looking for additional ways to recoup deficit financing on series. One of the best examples of this "corporate product synergy" is the animated series, produced by Warner Bros. in association with Steven Spielberg, entitled *Tiny Toon Adventures*. Prior to production, many of the media divisions were developing exploitation strategies. Tiny Toons became an overnight success in the U.S. and overseas, and is one of the most well recognized animated series of its time.

TOP RATED FEATURES FOR 1990 SPAIN

TITLE	STN.	RTG.	#VIEWERS	ORIGIN	RELEASE YEAR
EL GOLPE	TVE1	36.9	12,191,022	SPAIN	N/A
GHOSTBUSTERS	TVE1	35.9	11,761,528	U.S.	1984
ESTA CAZA ES UN RUINA	TVE1	35.1	11,596,338	SPAIN	N/A
THE SWARM	TVE1	35.1	11,596,338	U.S.	1978
TOOTSIE	TVE1	27.6	9,118,488	U.S.	1984

SOURCE: EURODIENCE/BARB

The following is an example of what corporate synergy looks like.

Notes:

1) Maintain and improve relations between ourselves and our clients. Several of our most im-

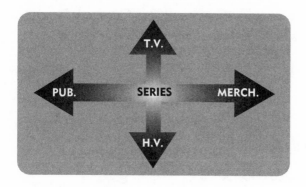

portant clients (RA12, TF1, Berlusconi, Beta Tau-rus, ARD & ZDF) are into co-producing with American companies.

2) Costs almost the same amount to produce in Europe as U.S. (A network quality program on film not utilized to reduce production budgets.)

3) Co-productions with end users increase the value of the program by 4 or 5 times more than if you license them a purely American product.

4) If a program is produced in Europe and obtains Euro quota status, it makes it more palatable for the European broadcasters, especially in France *(Dark Justice)*.

5) Problem - Not enough money in the international marketplace to justify an American company

like Warner Bros. to co-produce without a presale to a U.S. network or pay or basic cable service.

Notes:

A: License Fees Per Hour: (Acquired Product)

U.K. $40–60K

Italy $35–55 K

France $40–60 K

Germany $40–60 K

Spain $25–35 K

Local production costs $200–400 K per hour to produce

B: They have to program product other than local since there is not enough technical or creative talent to produce themselves.

WHY DO FOREIGN BROADCASTERS BUY U.S. PRODUCT?

A) LESS EXPENSIVE TO ACQUIRE THAN TO PRODUCE

B) U.S. PRODUCT PERFORMS BETTER THAN OTHER IMPORTS

C) NEED TO FILL ADDITIONAL AIRTIME (24 HOUR SERVICES)

FUTURE TECHNOLOGY

HIGH DEFINITION TELEVISION

PAY PER VIEW/CABLE

LASER DISK TECHNOLOGY

There are currently four standards of video signal available throughout the world. NTSC, PAL, SECAM, and the latest HDTV, which has become a hot political topic around the world.

Basically, HDTV is based on 1250+ lines per video, and is mastered digitally allowing up to 200 levels of brightness. Digital development led to the creation of a new type of tape made from metal. In addition, HDTV will be able to receive PP system.

Notes:

Many countries are designing systems to receive the HDTV signal:

The Europeans have developed the HD MAC system

The Japanese use the MUSE system

In the U.S., there are five contenders for the development rights to HDTV.

Ideally, the world's broadcasting community would like to convert to one standard, HDTV by the end of the century.

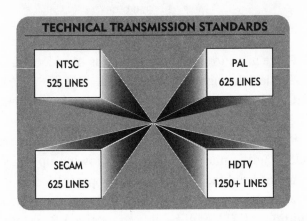

Pay per view is currently not available in foreign markets, but Europe's second Astra satellite will make channels available for pay per view within 1–2 years.

The pay per view window in the U.S. is currently 28–35 days after home video release. As pay per view's popularity and revenue increase, movies will probably be available on PP prior to video.

As more channels are designated for pay per view, it will be regarded as the "home video" of the future.

Note: Queens has 57 channels.

Laser disk technology will change the way you perceive your television. New technology allows one to interact with their television.

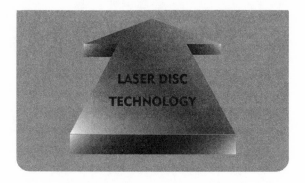

That's All Folks!

RAMPING UP THE AMERICAN ECONOMY—TWO TRANSCENDENT APPROACHES

Edward E. Barr

President and Chief Executive Officer
Sun Chemical Corporation and DIC Americas, Inc.

Remarks by Edward E. Barr
on the occasion of the annual
Joseph I. Lubin Memorial Lecture
9 February 1993

New York University
Leonard N. Stern School of Business

Good evening. Thank you for according me the honor of presenting this year's Lubin Lecture.

During the course of my comments, I will touch on several subjects that I hope will both pique your interest and give you cause for further thought.

In the late 1950s, the social commentator Paul Goodman wrote a book entitled *Growing Up Absurd*. In it, he attempted to sort out the causes and prescribe some solutions to the mounting strains upon society resulting from the increasing number of youth who were "beat," angry, alienated, delinquent, and refusing to cooperate with, much less join, the "system." Goodman's chief observation was that America at the time was not providing youth with enough "man's work" to do. Society should not be surprised, he noted, that a large proportion of our nation's youth was disaffected.

Considering the era in which he wrote, Goodman could not be expected to be sensitive to the negative reaction which use of a gender-specific phrase like "man's work" might cause today. Nonetheless, it is clear from its context that Goodman used the phrase in the gender-inclusive meaning of the German word—"menschen." Therefore, my references to "man" and "man's work" really should be understood as denoting a quality above and beyond gender.

To understand what Goodman meant by "man's work," consider some of the questions he posed:

- How can one obtain more meaning and honor in work?
- How is it possible to have a high standard of living of whose quality we are not ashamed?
- What is the best way to put wealth to some real use?
- How can we attain social justice for those who have been shamefully left out?

Goodman's responses focused on bringing out youth's capabilities: finding out ways to restore a worker's role in the production process; and using leisure to engage in community enterprises. He called for the conservation of human resources, for promoting "manly independence" and for providing opportunities to engage in activities which people "can enthusiastically and spontaneously throw themselves into and be proud of the results."

The world, Goodman felt, not only was "not manly enough . . . but not earnest enough . . . lacking in the opportunity to be useful." He called for a world—in tones as admirable as they were vague—where a worthy life is the product of "bona fide activity and achievement." "My stratagem," he continued, "assumes that the young really need a more worthwhile world in order to grow up at all."

Certainly, it was a heady, obscurely populist, and really guileless vision Goodman offered. While it reflected perceptions and longing which struck responsive chords among many people, Goodman and like-minded commentators seldom got beyond an idealistic yearning for a better world. They manifested their chagrin with the contemporary U.S. situation, as well as their impatience. They put forward illusory expectations regarding human aspirations. They identified their own likes and dislikes with what they regarded as the desirable course and texture of human activity.

Nonetheless, I find it important and useful to recall *Growing Up Absurd* because its concerns are fundamentally important. Goodman resonated many of the most salient contemporary problems we face.

The relative affluence and technological achievements of the period following World War II helped engender a degree of alienation which triggered Goodman's preoccupation with "man's work." He identified issues which agitated not only youth but society as a whole. Similarly, our even greater affluence today, our continued technological evolution, and the decompression resulting from recent drastic changes in international pressures, likewise function to provide the seedbed for simmering alienation, discontent, and an anger which, in this volatile age, might readily bubble to the surface.

Significant segments of our society feel a lessening of purpose, an absence of clear-cut challenges, a loss of defining moral beliefs, and a continuing collapse of our national purpose and sense of community. All of these negatives debilitate our intellectual and moral thrust—what the German philosophers referred to as the "Zeitgeist"—which also leaves many individual citizens bereft of a sense of personal purpose.

I realize that in the time allotted to me I cannot completely address such broad and deep issues. Therefore, I will instead focus my remarks on certain affirmative and pragmatic approaches that I believe to be two of the transcending aspects of our national interests: first, an industrial strategy to help maintain America's competitive economic position, and, second, an education strategy that reworks a major precept—the priority and purpose in educating our youth.

I will relate these themes to Goodman's preoccupation that society has meaningful outlets for its energies with self-esteeming vocations for its citizens. I will attempt some suggestions towards reinvesting society with "a more manly purpose." All of our citizens, not just youth, require such "challenges."

The very origins and ethos of our society have always demanded nationally unifying and virtuous purposes. The policies advocated will underscore

Goodman's laudable concerns, while avoiding quixotic courses of action.

In achieving an industrial strategy for a more competitive America, the central objective must be to reverse the long-term economic decline which has beset the United States in recent decades. Undergirding this objective is the creation and availability of jobs—meaningful and decently paying jobs.

We cannot overlook the fact that jobs are directly and fundamentally related to the concept of "man's work," particularly in a society like ours. Calvinism and its philosophical relatives have deep roots in our consciousness. Our individual senses of identity are implanted often in the work we do—its satisfactions and its economic and psychic rewards.

Not having a productive job is a major contributor to alienation, disaffection, and delinquency. It is clear that the myth of the attractiveness of welfare has been misunderstood and misrepresented by those who would use this to serve their own political ideologies. The overwhelming number of people want a decent-paying job.

Our economic decline, despite several bright notes and some recent upturns in the relevant indicators, reflects certain systemic problems. Gloomy news has become as persistent as overcast skies in Great Britain:

- The job creation boom of the 1980s turned out to be short-lived, and each week brings an announcement of significant employee lay-offs at some major firm. Last month, the *New York Times* reported that employment at Fortune 500 companies was down more than 3.6 million in the decade ended 1991.
- As a result of mounting global competition, our market share in a disturbing number of industries has fallen dramatically or is under serious challenge.
- Average real wages have seriously eroded.
- Corporate profits are hardly robust, with one of the consequences being cutbacks in both employee training and research and development. Such cutbacks mean corporate America is endangering future economic crop yields by skimping on the planting of seed corn.
- The recession that began in mid-1990 was *not* shallow at all. Total real economic output fell by 2.2 percent (not the more optimistic 1.6 percent earlier predicted by the Commerce Department). The decline, moreover, lasted not six but nine

months. Nearly three million *more* were unemployed than prior to the recession. And, an additional 6 percent of the nation's industrial capacity became idle.

• In our immediate northeast region, the economic downturn has been "extraordinarily deep." A month ago, the *New York Times* reported that 92 percent of the nation's job losses since the beginning of 1989 have been in ten states, all of them — with the exception of California—here in the Northeast. "For manufacturers," the *Times* commented, "the recession has turned into a long, relentless period of decline, beginning in the 1950s, into something closer to a collapse." Citing government data, it noted that "270,000 manufacturing jobs—24 percent of the region's total—have been eliminated since November 1987, with the pace of decline showing no signs of subsiding."

• The so-called "peace dividend" to be realized from a sharp decrease in defense spending could cause increased unemployment and further destabilization of the economy unless handled very adroitly. Furthermore, most competent observers agree that America has been on a long-term economic decline for reasons having nothing to do with reduced defense spending.

Unfortunately, I could expand these negative notes beyond the realm of economic factors, and cite a discouraging list of social and educational phenomena that likewise debilitate our society.

However, I shall not prolong this dark litany; we have all been living through it for far too long. *The bottom line is that our economy is not terribly strong, and our national debt keeps growing.*

Speaking as the CEO of a prominent Japanese-controlled company headquartered in northern New Jersey, and as one of only four western executives serving on any publicly owned Japanese board of directors, as well as a businessman who has enjoyed more than 30 years' association with Japanese businessmen, I would like to share with you my understanding of that nation's impact and role with respect to our economic situation.

Unlike some commentators, I do not believe Japanese industry is a "menace" to the United States, and certainly not in the dictionary definition as "showing an intent to do evil" to us. On the contrary, they are "worthy challengers." They demon-

strate, often through intelligent and determined application of some of our own discoveries and
techniques, how we might mend or change certain
of our ways.

For several years I served as the Board Chairman
of the New Jersey Commission on Science and
Technology. At the end of 1983, when the Commission issued its first study and recommendations, the
staff proposed having the top of each page of the
report bordered by a running cartoon. Prudence dis-
suaded them from printing a continuous strip of
drawings showing a Toyota automobile orbiting a
map of the United States. This explicit reference to
the Soviet Sputnik, and the way that earlier space
launching had shocked and energized the U.S. science and industrial communities, was deliberate.
Similarly, and correctly in my view, the Toyota
reference had been intended to depict Japanese economic competition as a stimulus to the United States
to "get off its duff."

I will not deny that Japan (and the European
industrialized nations for that matter) are in economic conflict with us. However, as the *New York
Times* quoted a Japanese professor a few years ago:
"The United States and Japan will have to learn to
live with constant conflict. We are both competi-

tive, jealous and powerful nations." But, he added, "conflict doesn't mean war."

My experiences as CEO of Sun Chemical Corporation, coupled with my years as a partner and director of Courtaulds, the British chemical and textile conglomerate, have sharpened my understanding of global trade and competition and have convinced me that Japan's economic progress is to that nation's credit. Our concerns should not be directed toward hoping they will falter, but rather toward improving our own efforts. In addition, several factors are operative in Japanese society which indicate its competitive potential may, in fact, be slackening.

To expect that Japan can continue its recent pace of growth—when, in effect, it was playing catch-up ball and could borrow cheaply and improve our once more advanced techniques and technologies—is to misunderstand the dynamics of economic development and their statistical artifacts. And the fact that the Japanese economy, like ours, is experiencing its own difficulties, should not be cause for anyone to gloat. Such a move would be an inaccurate and improper projection. We must all be aware that we live in a global economy, and that economic distress in Japan will hurt all of us.

At the same time, I do not wish to leave the impression that America's economic situation and prospects are unremittingly poor. Today, we remain the "wealthiest society in the history of mankind." This conclusion is based on 1988 data using the "only meaningful way to make international comparisons," which is purchasing power parity, or the exchange rate at which different currencies would each buy the same basket of goods. *The Economist Book of Vital World Statistics* found:

The American standard of living was far above other advanced nations. With the U.S. at 100, Canada rated 92.5 and Switzerland 87.0. Then came the Scandinavian nations and some small countries, including Kuwait. West Germany rated tenth at 78.6 and Japan twelfth at 71.5. Other developed nations trailed.

Nonetheless there *is* serious cause for concern. Nothing is *ordained*. We are not *predestined* to be able to provide decent standards of living for all of our people. Certainly we are far from achieving that goal at present. I strongly believe, moreover, that a sound and thriving U.S. economy is necessary not solely for reasons of economic health and well being. It is also the prerequisite for a society where

Paul Goodman's criteria for "man's work" can be fulfilled.

The current absence for many of our youth—and for all too many of our older work force as well—of rewarding employment and career opportunities is discouraging and destabilizing. Reinvesting our economy with opportunity, renewed growth and job creation is a distinct challenge worthy of inclusion in any sensible catalogue of "man's work."

It is fortunate that the recent presidential election constituted a national voice of confidence affirming that strengthening the economy is our chief priority. The campaign highlighted somewhat contrasting approaches. Candidate Clinton's domestic economic proposals centered on public investment in education, training, and infrastructure; President Bush's plan called for various tax credits and incentives, pushing most strongly for his long-advocated cut in the capital gains tax. While an oversimplification, it is not unfair to characterize the former president's programs as being aimed at increasing investment in *physical* capital, while President Clinton focused on increasing investment in *human capital*.

To be sure, during the campaign a host of additional weaknesses in our economy and industrial structure were noted. None of these were given much stress by the candidates, in keeping with the conventional political wisdom that complexity of issues will confuse voters. I dispute the validity of this so-called truism, and note it is the spiritual father of the 30-second sound byte. It is heartening that our new President is giving policy "wonkism" needed respectability, through his participation in various seminars and serious self-study sessions, and by taking detailed positions on complex issues.

Our choices for action cannot be limited to "either-or." Our problems are multi-causal in origin, and while they cannot be addressed with equal vigor, they all merit attention.

Overcoming the immediate, much less the structural, problems in our economy will prove extremely challenging. Addressing these defects through a workable policy will require serious dedication and a willingness to take action unavoidably displeasing to one or another segment of society. It will mean grasping the nettle of truth, in Harvard economist Gregory Mankiw's observation, that "prosperity tomorrow requires sacrifice today."

Many of the rash and politically inspired promises of the electoral campaign are coming home to roost. It was, therefore, good to hear Leon Panetta, the U.S. Budget Director, during his confirmation hearing, acknowledge that we must make compromises and prioritize our actions. His priorities, with which I concur, are preserving the keys to long-term growth through deficit reduction and public investment.

I also recognize that most of the measures I favor carry cost implications. However, because I believe these measures are investments which in time will result in higher revenues to the Treasury, we should give them priority over certain ongoing programs, as well as others proposed during the election campaign.

This isn't the occasion to lay out a well-balanced blueprint of action, which frankly will require compromise among the government, business, labor, and public sectors. But there are four points I will make both strongly and fervently:

First – the solutions will be neither quick nor simple.

Second – the time for action is now. A prime responsibility of the federal government is to ensure that the people's perception of the health of our economy is reasonably positive, and to take such actions as will reinforce that perception. The time is past for *debating* whether or not our United States are in economic decline.

Third – our economic health is an indispensable aspect of our national prestige, security and ability to provide world leadership.

Fourth – there is an additional element in the tapestry of necessary solutions with which I will conclude my remarks regarding the nation's economic situation. This element is the need for an *industrial policy* to encourage certain key technologies. A major aspect of this strategy is to further foster partnerships between industry, academia and government in support of the scientific and engineering research and development which must underpin these technologies.

I endorse a pertinent recommendation of the Democratic Leadership Conference (from which, as you know, President Clinton emerged as a national political figure). It calls upon the federal government to proactively stimulate economic growth; to assist the private sector in promoting the *development,* in addition to the research, of emerging technologies. I am aware that the two previous administrations fully embraced only the research, not the development, aspects of the concept. Indeed, many key economic advisors to Presidents Reagan and Bush were ideologically opposed to such a strategy.

Initially, I want to assert my belief in the importance of scientific and technological progress to society's cultural, political and economic development. Belief in the efficacy of research and development to improve our lives, in fact, led me to accept the Chairmanship of New Jersey's Science and Technology Commission.

When I left the Commission several years ago, we had secured the proceeds from public bond issues totaling $135 million for construction and major equipment purchases. Our annual operating budget had grown to $25 million. We had established eleven academically based research centers to work with industry to promote the state's economy in such selected fields as biotechnology, opto-electronics and supercomputing. We conducted a multifaceted program to support industry-targeted research. We initiated several mechanisms, including incubators, small business advisory and investment groups, to help transfer the technology developed under our program.

New Jersey's Science and Technology Program, while one of the largest and most ambitious in the nation, was paralleled by similar efforts in most of the rest of the states. In addition, federal agencies, led by the National Science Foundation, the National Institutes of Health, and the Departments of

Defense and Energy, provided significant encouragement and separate and collateral support.

The story since about 1990 is far from sanguine, however. The economic downturn, at a minimum, has crimped all of the state-based programs. More shocking is the news that U.S. private research spending subsequently began falling for the first time.

Last August's report, "The Competitive Strength of U.S. Industrial Science and Technology," from a prestigious panel appointed by the National Science Board, declared that scientific research by American business was in "a perilous state of stagnation." This report, from the policy-making parent of the National Science Foundation, echoed the mounting alarms that American spending on industrial research had slowed from an annual average growth of 7.5 percent in constant dollars in the first half of the 1980s, to *only fourteenths of one percent* between 1985 and 1991.

The cause of this downturn was found to be not a change in federal policy, but the general management practices of private industry, and external financial pressures in the corporate world. Mounting corporate debt was one contributor to the squeeze on research support, but even more significant, the panel found, was the "growing dominance of institutional investors in equity markets and their demand for short-term returns on their investments."

In addition to its finding that the U.S. today spends too few dollars on industrial research, the National Science Board's panel added that poor use is made of the money that *is* spent. Many top corporate managers, the report stated, "lacked the skills and insights to tie technology into business strategy." The panel foresaw, as a consequence of all these negative signs, impending declines in the American computer factory automation, motor vehicle, metals and electronics industries!

A revealing chart in the panel's report also depicted how unbalanced *government*-financed research spending in 1989 was with respect to the nation's needs in a post–cold war era. Whereas 65.5 percent of U.S. government-financed research went to military projects, Germany devoted only 19 percent, and Japan an even lower 9 percent to that purpose. Alternatively, Japan applied some 39 percent of such funds to energy research, Germany 9.5 percent, and the U.S. less than 4 percent. *Most disgracefully,* Germany provided 19 percent of government research funds to *industrial* development and Japan more than 8 percent, while the U.S.

invested a truly anemic *two tenths of one percent* of its federal research budget to the industrial sector!

I firmly believe that healthy economic growth in the long run is contingent on increasing productive capacity, which in turn derives to a significant degree from the fruits of R&D. Given that indispensable role of R&D in sustaining the nation's economic health, I would forcefully urge positive action on several of the National Science Board's recommendations, specifically:

- Enact a permanent tax credit to industry for expenditures on research and development.
- Place a moratorium on a Treasury Department regulation that induces American corporations to move research overseas.
- Sharply reverse priorities and shift the focus of the federal scientific research budget from the military to those commercial sectors closer to the civilian marketplace.
- Initiate a pilot federal effort to help improve industrial research practices, including a program to sharpen the understanding of future corporate leaders of both high technology and traditional industries.

But even all this is not enough, in my view, to reinvigorate the share and distribution of funding devoted to industrial research. They are necessary steps, but, in and of themselves, not a sufficient solution.

We likewise need an additional approach to R&D activity. We should forthwith establish an industrial policy centered around federal stimulus and support for collaborative research and development activities among companies *in select, targeted technological fields*. This is not a wholly new approach. Several such cooperative R&D projects already leverage the research investments of diverse American companies.

There is particular justification for government collaboration in such strategically important, high-development-cost, short-product-cycle, high-tech fields like aeronautics, computing, electronics, advanced molecular biology, and biomaterials.

A prudent constraint would be that industry research patronized by the federal government be a cooperative team effort with business. It should focus usually on generic, pre-competitive, pre-trade secret technologies like clean manufacturing methods which have a broad range of commercial applications. The research priorities essentially should be set by the industry partners. Both initially, and increasingly over the life of each project initiative, the majority of the money should also come from these industry collaborators. University researchers likewise should be brought into these collaborations, though not given the leadership role or prime funding benefits as they are in many of the state-financed programs.

At present, only a small portion of American industry engages in collaborative research and development. Some observers ascribe this to the absence of the sort of culture of cooperation found among our Asian competitors. Small companies, beset by great pressure even to survive, are especially laggard in this respect.

Military contractors in particular should be given incentives to join such R&D consortia, including specific assistance to retrain their employees to help in the shift to civilian production.

An interesting bill along these lines has been floating around Congress for some time. Representative Sander Levin of Michigan and Senator Joseph Lieberman of Connecticut have proposed providing a 50 percent tax credit to companies engaging in approved collaborative research projects.

Additionally, I strongly advocate ramping up federal support to selected research consortia. An evidently successful precedent is Sematech, the industry-run collaboration to increase American competitiveness in semiconductor manufacturing. Sematech has been credited with playing a major role in the nation's recent regain of market share in that field. We should explicitly help industrial firms to defray the costs of expensive lead-edge research. Such federal research support should include a special charge to promote commercial applications out of the basic research, to help ensure that this country derives the maximum harvest from its inventive genius.

If it hasn't been perfectly clear from my previous remarks, let me underscore that federal participation should be predicated on very significant matching support from industry, as well as from other governmental jurisdictions and academia, where applicable. Federal support, furthermore, should be extended only under realistic sunset and compliance-review provisions. Finally, a national civilian research and development instrumentality, analogous to the highly successful Defense Advanced Research Projects Agency (DARPA) should be established to identify, prioritize, and coordinate support to technologies critical to the future of our economy.

Even the critics of industrial policy have not contested DARPA's successes in support of industrial developments in computer graphics, semiconductors, supercomputing, and computer-controlled machine tools. Under similarly astute leadership, a civilian DARPA also can play a critical stimulative role in the commercial deployment of those technologies.

You will have discerned by now that I have crossed an ideological Rubicon. I have uttered the dreaded phrase "industrial policy," which was "verboten" in Washington for more than a decade. Notwithstanding that, our industrial policy should incorporate the following components:

One – Measured subsidies to select strategic industrial technologies.

Two – Regulatory systems designed to encourage business growth, even as they provide necessary control in society's behalf, including environmental and safety considerations.

Three – Product standards that facilitate productivity, while providing consumer protection.

I favor a national industrial policy not because I

favor a highly centralized, controlled, and meddle-some "picking of winners" from among individual private industrial firms. On the contrary, placing a government glove over the invisible hand of the free market is abhorrent to me. Competitive market principles are the best device to guide the distribution of resources. But let's not become hopelessly dogmatic about the matter.

Advocating certain muscular industrial policy measures, as I do, doesn't constitute a call upon the government to do anything and everything to redirect the market. For one thing, the United States must continue its role as the principal upholder of global free trade policies. We do not need an American version of Japan's MITI—a government agency to *direct* significant capital investment, other than R&D support, where it otherwise hasn't gone. Nor should the government ever bail out industries, much less individual companies, that cannot hack it in the marketplace, whether due to inefficiency, poor management, valid competition, or because their category of products is just no longer as in demand as in the past.

The critics of industrial policy should stop setting up straw men by charging its advocates with the equivalent of all-out war on the principles of laissez-faire. Purely and simply, I merely call for the federal government to help develop critical technologies, and to provide a fertile environment in which the industries which use them can grow. Senator Jeff Bingaman of New Mexico stated it succinctly when he said the government should "become a more active catalyst for the changes that are required." It is not a matter of picking winners or losers, Bingaman continues, "but when a choice has been made by industry, and when it's clear that a particular technology has the potential to be a winner, government should help it become one."

I cannot deny there are cogent critical arguments and reservations that have been raised about adopting an industrial policy. But they do not devastate me. Lack of a crystal ball in deciding what technologies are strategic, lack of objectivity, forming ego attachments with one's favorite projects, etc., are not disabilities confined to the public sector executive.

For example, may I mention the Edsel and its progeny in the auto industry. The argument that at least industry's failures don't break the public bank, flies in the face of reality. All those employee layoffs in the headlines lately don't occur in an economic vacuum. Most significantly, we are not talking about government becoming the majority stockholder in these technologies. We are talking government as a "catalyst."

I could characterize my approach as an *enlightened* free market approach; or perhaps as a *market-driven* economic strategy. The point is not whether to prefer one or the other phrase. Rather, the essential point is: *are we willing to forego ideology and modify past practices when we make our decisions* as to how to maintain our standard of living and how to maintain American economic hegemony?

Supporters of the kind of industrial consortia proposed, both in the U.S. and abroad, cite many positive outcomes in their behalf. Among them:

- They stimulate a sense of purpose and commitment and have a real, even if intangible, positive effect on the industry involved.
- In bringing companies together to overcome technological obstacles, they have promoted useful mergers, alliances and other forms of cooperation.
- They effectively diffuse ideas throughout an industry by encouraging exchanges of scientists and engineers among the consortium members.
- They are able to achieve economies of scale by engaging in broader-scale investigations over

longer periods of time than are possible for single companies.

- By coordinating national R&D initiatives, they help avoid unproductive and duplicative efforts. For example, Alcatel, a French company, credits *RACE,* the European community's R&D consortium for communications technology, with helping create continent-wide standards as well as breakthroughs in such areas as fiber optics. Interestingly, a *RACE* scheme to establish an integrated European broadband telecommunications network, is cousin to Vice President Gore's long espousal of a similar nationwide infrastructure in the United States to link sophisticated computers in industry, educational institutions, laboratories, and hospitals.
- After more than a decade of experience, federal and state government-supported industry and academic collaborative research has become well established, generally respected, and a not very costly mechanism for fostering economic growth.

I obviously believe it is entirely plausible to construct industrial policies which can, in a reasonable proportion of the cases, increase productivity and competitiveness. In fact, both the United States and

Japanese economic growth after World War II were grounded in similar tactics.

Japan's take-off was engineered via the integration of an intricate and informal network of cooperation. Cooperation—not control—between the governmental and industrial sectors, between political and economic affairs. This fuzzing of the boundaries between the private and public spheres goes beyond anything the United States would approve, or that most of us here would advocate.

On the other hand, as stated earlier, we should not view the choices as "either/or." After 1945, America *itself* successfully switched from war-driven, military priorities to an economy heavily focused on automobiles, housing, and consumer products. This happened not magically or automatically, but as a consequence of a little-known *deliberate* effort.

A governmental initiative was launched as early as 1944, when the national leadership became confident of our ultimate victory over the Axis powers. A small group, including such eminent economists as Alvin Hansen and Gardiner Means, was formed. Working out of Washington with the directors of our factories then producing the guns, tanks, and planes, the group anticipated and planned for the civilian products a war-rationed population would demand.

Estimates of the amount of steel, lumber, rubber, glass, and other strategic materials were prepared. Like the coach who recruits a championship college basketball squad—by persuading individual high school stars to come to his institution and join talented peers on a likely winning team—they rallied private industry. The group encouraged companies to make investments, start production line changes, order materials, and undertake the myriad tasks necessary to a flourishing civilian economy.

They did not take a "command economy" approach—planning down to every nut and bolt, centralized decisions, production quotas, and all that persuasive prattle dear to socialized government bureaucracy. Instead, their approach consisted of broad surmises of what a post-Depression, post-war population would want for itself and its children. It consisted of reasonable estimates of the extent of demand in several, *limited* key areas. It calculated the amount of subsidiary materials and goods that would be required to build those products. It targeted certain technologies and industries as constituting economic *pulsars*.

Government investments, subsidies, and tax dollars, on the whole, were *not* offered. What industry received was encouragement; intelligent analyses of future business prospects; and assurances that the sources of necessary supplies were similarly alerted and tooling up. In short, some broad industrial objectives were identified, and a framework provided for unleashing free competitive talent and energy.

This account of the post–World War II effort led by Hansen and Means harbors some analogy to our current situation. With the demise of the Soviet Union and the end of the cold war, we must prevent further deflation as we convert a heavily defense-oriented economy to civilian applications. As the *New York Times* observed last July:

With the Cold War over, the need to convert from military to civilian production is one of the major engines behind the push for an industrial policy. The new defense conversion initiative in Congress aims to ensure that the talents of thousands of research engineers who helped build the world's most sophisticated military machine are used to develop commercial technologies. There is also a push to get military companies to adopt flexible manufacturing techniques so that factories that make fighter aircraft today might make high-speed trains tomorrow.

I don't mean to imply that the Hansen and Means effort was the sole successful use of industrial policy in our history. Do any of you recall hearing of the National Advisory Committee for Aeronautics (NACA)? It was first created in 1915 and in 1958 became a part of NASA. During its existence, NACA was characterized as "arguably the most important and productive aeronautical research establishment in the world. . . . It published 16,000 reports sought after and exploited by aeronautical engineers, . . . developed wind tunnels, as well as other equipment and techniques, that revolutionized aeronautical research."

What is most poignant and pertinent is that NACA was founded by the U.S. government as a reaction to European efforts to exploit the Wright brothers' invention. The authorizing legislation noted that despite aviation's birth in the U.S., by 1915 we were "lagging . . . behind the European nations that were pursuing aeronautical research under government auspices, while in the United States it was scattered, uncoordinated, and wasteful for lack of a central body to provide continuity and prevent duplication."

NACA's founders believed aviation's future in the U.S. depended on a healthy and prosperous aircraft manufacturing industry. NACA was a booster of industry, "limited only by its need to be fair and impartial in disbursing favors and assistance." With the discovery on the eve of World War II that German advances, particularly in the area of jet propulsion, posed increasing danger, industry representatives were added to NACA committees and working groups, changing the organization's character to become even more industry-responsive. Thereafter, industry representatives actively used NACA laboratory facilities.

NACA had a structure and independent status within the federal hierarchy which made it an ideal forum for all branches of American aeronautics to debate and develop a national research program, and without undue interference from the rest of government.

A study of NACA prepared by AT&T/Bell Laboratory personnel in 1991 credited the organization with such dramatic innovations as: the NACA Cowling, the low-drag airfoil, the transonic wind tunnel, the X-Series research aircraft of the 1940s and 1950s; and such incremental developments over the years as solutions to the problems of aircraft icing, improved ducts and inlets, techniques of streamlining, and proper engine placement on wings and fuselage. The Bell Lab's study, prepared expressly for its then president, Ian Ross, concluded that "NACA contributed significantly to every United States aircraft built during this country's rise to world preeminence in aviation."

It is not an arcane endeavor to identify those scientific and technological fields which will be important to future world affairs and the American economy. Several prestigious national level groups have made their overlapping recommendations. The Commerce and Defense Departments have identified what they regard as tomorrow's critical technologies.

Again there are overlaps. It would not be an error to provide the kind of support I have outlined to many of the technologies on their lists. A mere reading is like a roll call of our future style of life: biotechnology, advanced sensors, advanced semiconductor devices, robotics, sensitive radars, air breathing propulsion, super-computers, flexible computer integrated manufacturing, and the optoelectronic fields of optical fibers and lasers.

Clyde Prestowitz, a former Reagan administration official, now heading a Washington-based research group, has stated: "Industrial policy is an idea whose time has come." If even a Reagan Republican is coming around to the concept, then I trust we Americans can now get on with the job of putting it to work for our economy.

This brings me to my second and last theme this evening—American education and the workplace as learning environments. I shall not address the issues comprehensively, but merely endorse those that are profoundly important and require the nation's most serious attention. I personally grappled for years with these issues, while serving as a member, and subsequently as chairman, of the New Jersey Board of Higher Education.

Economist Lester Thurow, in his book *Head to Head,* declared that in the 21st century, "the education and skills of the work force will end up being the dominant competitive weapon." I agree, which is one reason for focusing my concerns on an educational concept which has long been discussed; one which has been extremely successful in certain other societies; and one which is not unknown— albeit little used here in the United States.

The most meritorious characteristic of this concept is its proven ability to help youth who do not go on to college to make a safe passage from adolescence to adulthood. Its practical relationship with Paul Goodman's concern with "man's work"

is the sense of purpose it lends to academic schooling, and its provision of the theoretical and practical
skills necessary to survive in an industrial world.
"Man's work" after all could be defined as adult
work.

The concept I am endorsing is *youth apprenticeships*—especially:

- Why they can better exploit our actual work
  places as learning environments.
- How they can provide mentor relationships and
  adult role models for our often unoriented youth.
- And, speaking as a CEO of a company that has
  experienced the difficulties in hiring the routinely
  ill-prepared products of our secondary schools,
  how they can instill in the nation's future employees the flexible vocational skills, and dependable
  attitudes, essential in today's world.

Some of the concepts, even the phraseology, I will
employ are drawn from the various writings of Ste-
phen Hamilton, Professor of Human Development
at Cornell University. Hamilton has become the
nation's outstanding advocate of the "necessity of
helping young people make the crucial connection

between school learning, community participation, and a satisfying, constructive life's work."

In fact, while still Governor of Arkansas, Bill Clinton gave this tribute to Hamilton's landmark 1990 book, *Apprenticeship for Adulthood:*

Too many of our young people aren't moving from school to good jobs with a good future today. Apprenticeship is an idea which has worked in other countries. We ought to try it here.

What's more, several bills in Congress and various state legislatures, including one passed in 1990 in Arkansas, push the concept. The Federal Labor Department and a number of private foundations are funding a variety of pilot projects.

But the results are meager, with the Labor Department reporting that fewer than one thousand people are enrolled nationwide in the distinct type of program denoted as *youth apprenticeships*. Since there are few people who haven't encountered the word "apprenticeship," and since everyone has his or her own image of what it entails, *let me list the programs to which I am not referring.*

1. Cooperative education at the *collegiate* level, made notable at institutions like Cincinnati and

Northeastern Universities, and a score of community colleges. These commence *after* high school, or, at best, in *late* adolescence.

2. Vocational education and work-study programs in our high school systems. Let it suffice to say that these tired and conventional programs, too often captive of old-line bureaucracies, and which train for narrow occupational fields and *specific* jobs, do little more than give the concept of apprenticing a bad odor.

3. Traditional apprenticeship programs, which currently prepare some 300,000 young people *already out of high school,* to be licensed carpenters, electricians, bricklayers, and similar craftsmen. The International Brotherhood of Electrical Workers, for example, began developing a full apprenticeship program in 1957, and has a commendable record for turning out highly skilled, well-paid journeymen.

One critical characteristic of all these programs, however, is that the average enrollee enters in his late 20s, sometimes pushing 30.

The "Youth Apprenticeship" concept, in contrast to the existent programs, is designed to steer non-college-bound students, *as early as their second year in high school,* into skilled jobs. This sharply diminishes the risk that non-college-bound students will drift, having received no occupational skills or work-place socialization before or after high school graduation.

The idea seems, to me at least, so attractive that one wonders why it hasn't caught on long ago. Aside from the resistance of interests adverse to change, or the diminution of their empires, there appear to be two formidable constraints:

- It seemingly goes against the grain of the American belief in universal upward mobility;
- U.S. companies, which would assume substantial financial as well as oversight responsibilities under the program, historically have competed by simplifying work procedures and lowering costs.

Hamilton notes that "youth apprenticeship runs against the U.S. industrial mindset of viewing labor as a cost to be minimized." On the contrary, he says, "You have to view workers as an investment, and when you do, you try to get as much output from them as possible, and you train them accordingly."

I firmly believe a refocus is long overdue in U.S. secondary education to engage the interests and involve our less academic youth. "The most glaring structural problem with American education," the *Economist* declared last November in a special survey of the issues, "is that it does not know what to do with pupils who are not bound for college. . . . In importing the German university system, in the late 19th and early 20th centuries, America made the disastrous mistake of forgetting to import the apprenticeship system as well. For apprenticeships smacked of class-stratification, and America was hypnotized by upward mobility."

The consequence for our country is that about half of our 18-year-olds are stuck with the stark choice of either going to college, or with poor preparation going directly into the job market. This wasn't so formidable for the latter group while low-skill, but still relatively high-paying assembly line type jobs were reasonably plentiful. What has broken down in the scheme of things is that higher basic qualifications, more precise skills, and the maturation that comes with familiarity with workplace practices, are now required in our increasingly sophisticated, information technology-dominated industrial culture.

In fixing our deficiency, we are well-advised to look abroad. Most of us are aware—at least vaguely—that the world's most successful and extensive apprenticeship system is found in Germany. A quick summary of that system is in order.

Youth in Germany can choose to enter a vocational school track and begin their three-year, sometimes longer, apprenticeships as early as the age of 15. This decision is preceded by extensive counseling and evaluation of alternative apprenticeship career tracks. It is not inflexible and it permits a change to another career track by the 70 percent of German students in the program.

While clearly not a universal option chosen by all German youth, 85 percent of those who do not enter the academic collegiate preparatory track go into apprenticeships. Interestingly, some 20 percent of Germans graduate from college, very close to the 24 percent that actually completes baccalaureate education in our country, where approximately 50 percent begin to pursue some form of college education.

The standards are set mainly by industry and are uniform throughout the country. The student enters into a contract with a firm that provides a highly structured program of on-the-job training, generally for three days a week, and state-provided theoretical training for two days a week.

The apprentices work in real time, with real responsibilities, alongside adult colleagues, and acquire from these mentors their work habits and attitudes. Adolescent boredom fades during the program, in large part because the students are given adult-type assignments, and see the linkage between learning theory and facts, and earning a living. The traumatic school-work transition is neutralized, and a culture is fostered in which training is respected and skilled work revered.

The cost of the German programs is divided between the local government groups which provide the theoretical schooling, the employers who are assessed a percentage of their payroll expenses, and the apprentices themselves who work for only a nominal salary.

Successful graduates receive a journeyman's certificate—the ticket to adult employment—only when they pass a demanding written and practical exam at the end. By 18 or 19, when they assume adult jobs, they possess very high levels of academic and vocational skills, and as anyone who has visited German companies is aware, they know what it means to work.

The German firms are not required to take on apprentices; they can pay into a government fund instead. But most do participate. In part, it is a matter of corporate pride, but more importantly their participation stems from the conviction, after years and years of positive results, that the programs prepare a highly skilled work force. Moreover, youth who complete the apprenticeships successfully all appear to get employed subsequently, and even those who don't finish the program clearly derive considerable benefit.

As an employer who would be directly tithed should these recommendations come to pass, let me say a bit more about the European taxes on corporations for worker training. Whereas in Germany corporations are required to spend 2–3 percent of payrolls for training; in Sweden and Ireland 2.5 percent; in France 1.5 percent; in the U.S. employers only spend an average of 1 percent. And 70 percent of that very often goes for comfortable seminars for executives and marketing staff rather than production-based workers. President Clinton's campaign recommendation for increases in training support, it is estimated, would cost private industry billions of dollars a year, even with his seemingly modest call for a rise to 1.5 percent of payrolls. So we *are* talking about real money that should be put to work where it will have the most benefit.

I don't want to leave the impression that the

German system of apprenticeship is without faults. Many observers recoil because of what they perceive as caste-influenced characteristics. A specific concern also resides in the fact that many small firms cannot afford the price tag to train a recruit.

Therefore, some fine tuning appears to be in order. In Denmark, for instance, they give greater emphasis to theoretical training (because it lasts a lifetime) than to practical skills (which are soon outdated). They have constructively cut the number of apprenticeship categories from 300 to 80, while there still are 375 officially defined occupations in Germany. The Danes also have engineered the financing procedures such that the participating educational institutions are forced to compete for students. We have this program in our Danish chemical company, and I know it works!

I will not recount the many reasons, or cite the dreary examples, of the difficulty of importing foreign models to a distinct culture like our own. Nonetheless, we would be wise to take some leaves from the book of German experience.

The *Economist,* for instance, has acknowledged that the Germans have demonstrated "an unrivaled ability to churn out skilled workers, which gives them a vital advantage in the age of human capital, enabling firms to exploit information technology and flexible production." In an ultimate tribute, the British publication likened the result to "the medieval master craftsmen certainly built to last." William Northdurft, in a German Marshall Fund-supported study, "Reinventing Public Schools to Create the Work Force of the Future," arrives at the same conclusion. Lester Thurow, in discussing "The Coming Economic Battle Among Japan, Europe and America," points to the advantage countries like Germany derive from the fact that "the bottom two-thirds of their work force is better skilled" than our own. Incidentally, Japan, which does not have a broad-based program of alternative secondary school apprenticeships, more than compensates for this with the most comprehensive "in-company" program of worker training in the world.

An especially remarkable fact about the German experience was reported recently by another enthusiastic supporter, Ray Marshall, who served as Labor Secretary under President Carter. "Fully one-third of German university-trained engineers came up first through their apprenticeship system and then attended university, a path that would be unthinkable for most U.S. engineers." Marshall's point is doubly significant because it disabuses those who decry the German approach by claiming it tracks students into irrevocable life decisions.

There is still another hang-up in American educational philosophy and preoccupation which inhibits the adoption of youth apprenticeships. This is the egalitarian assumption that all youth are capable of learning at levels that most other societies reserve for the school system's most achieving students. This was a fundamental premise of the monumental, influential, and otherwise excellent 1983 study, "A Nation at Risk," which galvanized much-needed attention on the educational crisis in the United States.

One of its praiseworthy recommendations was to toughen up the standards of our schools, increase the rigor and number of required courses, and promote a greater student mastery of basic academic knowledge and skills. I am absolutely in accord with these objectives, but unfortunately the "Risk" study mistakenly overlooked, and its prescriptions for action did not provide for, the fact that *all* students do *not* respond uniformly to tough academic curricula, programs, and schools.

Not all youth can learn the same material in the same way. In addition, as important as the academic curriculum is for collegiate preparation, the school environment only very tangentially addresses the need to instill what Hamilton refers to as "worker virtues." Moreover, particularly in our inner cities but by no means confined to those settings, there are multiple non-school influences on youth which wash over and many times overwhelm our schools.

Youth apprenticeships incorporate the premise that the effects of our schools must be buttressed by what happens in other spheres of life as well. Two of these, the family and community at large, are receiving much attention of late and also should be necessary components of a total strategy. What youth apprenticeships bring into play is that additional societal sphere—known as the work place.

Without jettisoning concern or attention to student mastery of necessary knowledge and skills, Hamilton points out, a major function of youth apprenticeships is captured in the German word "arbeitstugende," meaning "the virtues of work." The apprenticeships help youth internalize "the need to be punctual, diligent, responsible, and receptive to supervision." Hamilton concurs that if such virtues "are yoked to passivity and subordination, they deserve to be stigmatized," but he rejects any facile dismissal of them. The "virtues of work" are as important, he insists, to middle class youth who have been known to coast through school, watch TV excessively, and spend much of their time "having fun," as they are to those raised in socially and economically disadvantaged families.

No one can guarantee that participants in such youth apprenticeships will refrain from drug and alcohol use, premature motherhood, delinquency, or the criminal and other negative behavior that is increasingly so disruptive among our high school youth. Nor will these programs absolutely eradicate the situation where many high school students drop out formally, or mentally, even when they succeed in graduating officially. But my response to this disheartening situation, which has not only eluded solution but gotten much worse, is a bit of wisdom from the Torah which is loosely translated as "What is the alternative?"

Our high schools for non-college-bound youth essentially serve as warehouses, or like holding patterns over an overcrowded airport. They keep them for some additional years out of the adult job market, until they are dispirited enough to be eased into whatever employment is available.

This is all a waste! Under the prevailing regimen, too many non-college-bound youth are prepared with nothing that comports with the requirements of a dynamic, fast-changing, increasingly technological society. Restless and dispirited, is it any wonder that their behavior and work attitudes are unattractive to prospective employers?

My final argument for youth apprenticeships derives from the changing nature of manufacturing today. In the past, manufacturing flourished by separating complex tasks into their simplest components, with omnipotent managers making the strategic decisions and telling the workers what to do. The workers became semi-skilled cogs operating single-purpose equipment in the industrial machine, and their educational preparation was not of great moment.

This has all changed. The key to competitive success for advanced societies like ours is "flexible specialization," not mass production. The developing countries now can, and do, run mass production machinery at much lower cost. As a consequence they are weaning away more and more of our so-called smokestack industries. The alternative long-term markets for the production of countries like the United States are upscale. Our work force, using multi-purpose equipment, must become proficient at supplying in timely fashion, on short production runs, a variety of high quality goods to essentially affluent customers. The work force must have highly developed, craft-like skills, and the judgment to participate in decision making and quality control.

This means that for the U.S. to be competitive, we must not only reorganize production, but begin to generate large cadres of highly motivated, skilled, and flexible workers. Amidst all the calls for educational reform going back to the decade of the 1950s, and despite all the increased investments in education made by the nation, we seem to have missed that target.

A better prepared, more sophisticated work force does not mean more academic preparation for college, or college attendance itself, as important as these objectives are for other youth. Indeed, it would be "criminal" to steer a still higher proportion of the educational dollar to higher education. Given the cost to society of U.S. collegiate education— tuition, endowment contributions, rich subsidies from federal, state, and local government—non-college youth are already relatively neglected. They "have been consistently overlooked and under-trained." According to Hamilton, a large number receive "no public support during their transition to adulthood."

There are clear class and racial overtones to this discrepancy, moreover, when we consider the disparate income and racial composition of the college, as opposed to the non-college-going populations. It is not unfair to conclude, therefore, that the national overwhelming emphasis on college education has undercut a necessary attention to work force preparation. Richard Hyse, a former economics professor at SUNY Oswego, has written:

First, it degrades any type of blue-collar work to a non-honorific status, making any apprenticeship system by definition fit only for the intellectually less endowed, the dropouts, the inner-city unreachables. With this de-emphasis also comes an abandonment of craft codes, which acted as quality controls and a source of personal pride.

More money in itself is not the answer, especially if these investments aren't in the right place. The sociologist James Coleman has conclusively shown that the differences in expenditures between schools are almost wholly unrelated to differences in academic performance. The relationship between money and results is further made equivocal by the fact that the German government spends a lower proportion of its budget on education (9.1 percent) than any other European community government, but can still point to an educational system envied by most of the world.

I think the Germans must be doing something right in this sphere, and will therefore sum up why I think we should emulate them:

First – We would be steering a precious and fragile portion of our youth on the path towards "man's work." It has been estimated that if Americans were involved in youth apprenticeships to the same relative extent as their German counterparts, not 300,000 but 6,000,000 would be enrolled.

Second – Institution of a significant youth apprenticeship movement would set in motion an overdue shakeup, not only of the secondary school system and its vocational education component, but would inevitably result in a long-needed, many-fold increase of corporate investment in human resources.

Third – In addition to financial participation, these apprenticeships would draw industry into playing a more crucial role in providing focus, content, and a supportive setting for the upbringing of our youth.

Fourth – Because the apprenticeships commence early in adolescence, before hormonal changes run the full course, before young people get discouraged over future prospects, or get caught up in some of the more pernicious distractions of contemporary life, these apprenticeships can have significant beneficial effects on the behavior of problem youth.

And, finally, by explicitly dealing with their socialization and internalization of "worker virtues," youth apprenticeship will help its participants both build more satisfying lives for themselves, and contribute a vital, better prepared resource to society.

The great challenge facing the nation is to prepare a changing population of young people to prepare to do a new kind of work. Failure will imperil our economic health, social progress, and democracy itself. It is not a college education which can prepare such workers. Sadly, for the non-college-bound American youth, neither is it the traditional high school diploma. Moreover, the forms of education that are reasonably effective with advantaged youth are seldom able to assist large numbers of disadvantaged youth achieve similar goals. Poor and minority youth need more support and encouragement.

The situation clearly calls for a dramatic change. That's why I believe the youth apprenticeship approach is required "to connect schools to work places and to provide young people with clearer paths from school to work." My purpose has not been to provide a precise, technical prescription for the organization of an apprenticeship system, but rather to make a case for its serious adoption as a fundamental and major aspect of U.S. secondary education.

Let me conclude my remarks by sharing Erik Erikson's story about Sigmund Freud, who was asked what a healthy person ought to be able to do well. His response was "to love and to work." Unfortunately, lack of time prevented me this evening from dealing with the first necessity. You have heard a great deal, however, about "work," particularly with respect to Paul Goodman's assertion that a worthy life and world is the product of bona fide "manly" activity and achievement.

As a businessman, I am all too aware that American industry will sink or swim, depending on what happens in society at large. Fortunately, we find ourselves at a point in time when the quadrennial rites of American politics have brought us a new leader. This president is representative of the generation which followed right behind the one Paul Goodman anguished over—a president who comes to office with a mandate to make changes.

President Clinton's philosophy and proposals appear to me to be congruent with the recommendations I shared this evening with you. I hope you will judge my concerns important, and my thoughts as to how to address them, significant. Ladies and gentlemen, I thank you for your attention and patience.

TELEVISION IN THE NINETIES: REVOLUTION OR CONFUSION?

Shelly Schwab

President of MCA TV Universal Studios

Remarks by Shelly Schwab
on the occasion of the annual
Joseph I. Lubin Memorial Lecture
1 March 1994

New York University
Leonard N. Stern School of Business

In 1958, I came to NYU not full of confidence. I thought it was a long shot that I would be accepted, and, if I were, I wasn't confident I could get through and graduate.

It was here that I learned a most important lesson: If you dedicate yourself to a goal, develop a discipline to succeed, have the desire to sacrifice for that success, and put passion into your work, you will achieve your goal. It's a lesson that has served me well throughout my life. I will always be indebted to NYU for setting that tone.

I appreciate Dean Diamond's invitation to deliver the Lubin Lecture this year and consider it an honor and a privilege to be here this evening.

Now let's talk television.

Television in the nineties: What does the future hold for it?

- *Where do the real opportunities lie?*
- *With dozens of cable channels now available to the average home, and hundreds more on the way, how many do we actually watch?*

What is signal compression? Multiplexing? Video on demand? Interactivity? What are the underlying questions and challenges posed by the coming electronic or information "superhighway"? Beyond entertainment, what bearing will it have on our lifestyles?

Television in the nineties: revolution or confusion?

Although most of us in this room have spent our entire lives with television, it's still really a medium in its infancy. Yet, even in just four short decades, it's remarkable how many moments have touched, molded, and reshaped our lives.

However, even with its rich and colorful history,

in terms of real practical potential television hasn't even scratched the surface.

Once upon a time it was a medium of limited options on limited channels. For the three networks—ABC, CBS, and NBC—the underlying strategy was not so much to "entice the viewer" as to schedule the "least objectionable programming." But the day of targeting the passive viewer is over; no longer is a family of four sitting down to watch *Bewitched* considered making optimum use of the medium.

We're entering an age of audience fragmentation where programmers will find that their success depends on the aggressive pursuit of an individual viewer, with almost limitless options—500, 600, even 1,000 channels.

When I was growing up, I thought I had a big choice—seven channels to choose from! But it was television, and it was new, and it was exciting. But today's viewers aren't as easily wooed. For broadcasters, the coming electronic age is the technological equivalent of Columbus setting sail for the New World: It's uncharted territory, but where there's great danger, there's also great opportunity—opportunity best realized by understanding the dynamics that brought us to this point.

**Let's look back for a few moments at the
growth of television by decade.**

I can remember in the fifties when television watching was considered an "event." Milton Berle was
the talk of the country, but for my family to watch
it, we had to go to a neighbor's house—we didn't
own a TV. And we weren't alone: the same was
true all over the country. But in just a five-year
span, television penetration in terms of households
went from almost nothing to two-thirds of the
country.

In the sixties, the television terrain became more
colorful, literally, with network schedules being
converted to all-color lineups, and many of us getting our first color sets. The sixties were also the
decade of the "demographic"—as ratings analysis
turned from being strictly quantitative to qualitative
as well. Advertisers began looking past raw numbers of households to find just who were their viewers—by age, sex, income.

By the seventies, the networks were aggressively
programming for young, urban viewers. Gone were
such longtime favorites as Jackie Gleason, Ed Sulli-
van, Red Skelton, even Lassie, and the silly rural

sitcoms of the sixties such as *Green Acres* and *The Beverly Hillbillies*. Instead, they were replaced by such landmark series as *All in the Family, M*A*S*H*, Mary Tyler Moore Show,* starting a new era in television comedy featuring story lines more sophisticated and relevant than anything that preceded it.

The question as we entered the eighties was: Where are the audiences going? The terrain of television began shifting. Instead of having the three major networks, with all other options almost an afterthought, the television landscape began taking on the look it has today . . . with the networks being just one of the viewers' alternatives.

First, there was the phenomenal growth of the independent stations (stations not affiliated with any of the big three networks). In 1975, there were only 102 of these so-called "indies" throughout the country. By 1985, there were 300, and there are now more than 430. This not only provided a major new alternative for viewers but, in effect, created a gold rush among program producers. Fulfilling the need of these independent stations is what transformed syndication into what it is today . . . now a major competition to the networks. Today many of the most popular and watched series are not on the networks but in syndication, i.e., *Oprah, Donahue, Star Trek, A Current Affair, Wheel of Fortune, Jeopardy,* and *Baywatch.* As a result, the amount of advertising expenditures for nonnetwork or syndicated programs has gone from $25 million annually in 1980 to $1.5 billion today.

A second new programming front was cable. In 1980 (and remember, this was only 14 years ago) cable penetration stood at just 18 percent of all households. CNN and MTV were launched and are now staples of daily life, and by 1985 cable penetration had jumped to 43 percent. It now stands at over 60 percent.

But, in addition to these changes from without, the eighties also brought the networks change from within: All three networks were sold—ABC to Capital Cities, NBC to General Electric, and CBS to Laurence A. Tisch of the Loews Corporation. And television's founding fathers, William Paley, David Sarnoff, Leonard Goldenson, visionaries who shaped each network's philosophy, were replaced by corporate entities run by bottom-line investors.

Meanwhile, another visionary and entrepreneur on a global scale, Rupert Murdoch, was buying both 20th Century Fox and the Metromedia stations and forming the Fox Broadcasting Company (later to become the fourth network). Ted Turner was adding to his Turner broadcasting empire by starting up additional cable channels and, more recently, acquiring Hollywood production companies.

Another critical change facing television, and Madison Avenue in particular, was the skyrocketing number of VCRs. Viewers were increasingly zapping through commercials when playing back tapes. With 55 percent of all homes having remotes by 1988, "grazing" or "channel hopping" during commercials became the advertisers' other big nightmare. (And a woman's nightmare as well, as men more than women are usually the zapping "culprits.")

This brings us to the nineties: With so many new entertainment alternatives coming into the field, what are the ramifications for the networks, the program suppliers, the advertisers, the viewers?

For the three major networks, their diminishing share of the audience pie is down to 60 percent and on any given night as low as 50 percent. Ten years ago it was 80 percent.

Fox, for example, as the upstart network, has already siphoned off a significant number of the big three networks' most demographically desirable viewers—the 18- to 34-year-olds—by aggressively programming for them with such series as *In Living Color, Beverly Hills 90210,* and *The Simpsons.*

In addition, more competition is on the way from Paramount and Warner, who are now engaged in a race to sign up as many affiliates as possible for their proposed fifth and sixth networks. It prompted one network insider to wonder, "If networks are a dying business, how come everyone is in such a rush to start one?"

The answer is, of course, that the networks may not necessarily be dying, but to survive they may have to reconfigure significantly. Based on new FCC regulations, there is now a strong possibility that one or two of the networks could be bought by film studios, or vice versa. Networks that were until recently pure buyers of programs will increasingly become suppliers, producing not only their own programming but, in select instances, that of their competition. For example, Fox, which has its own network, is now producing the Emmy Award–winning series *Picket Fences* for CBS. The old definition of mixed emotions was "watching your mother-in-law drive off a cliff in your new Cadillac." The new equivalent may be producing the number one series in prime time—for your competition.

Other changes facing the networks? The news and sports divisions may not survive on all three. Networks will continue to buy stakes in more and more advertiser-supported cable channels such as ESPN, Lifetime, and A&E; again, under the theory that as long as someone has to be in competition with me, why not let it be me?

What are the programming trends of the nineties? Or to be more pragmatic, I suppose, in which directions are the economic realities of the business forcing network programmers to turn?

Sitcoms and dramas will continue to be staples of the networks' lineup. On the other hand, "action-hours" series such as the *A-Team* and *Magnum P.I.* that once accounted for 21 percent of the networks' lineups will continue to be conspicuous by their absence. With only the occasional exception, they just don't make 'em like they used to. Why? Strictly economics—the dollars involved don't make any sense. Exploding buildings and crashing car scenes are just too expensive to produce.

Action-hours cost between $1.3 to $2 million per episode to produce versus $1 million for dramas and $700,000 for reality programming. Incidentally, if big-budget action series are endangered, conversely, do you know what the fastest-growing form of programming on television is? Infomercials! As a start-up business, it's gone from grossing nothing to $1 billion a year, virtually overnight (and growing).

So where do we stand in 1994 and beyond?

- *There are now 94 million TV homes, reaching 98 percent of the country (1950: 4 million TV homes/ 10 percent of the country).*
- *65 percent of TV homes have two or more sets.*
- *61 percent of TV homes have cable.*
- *The average home receives 35 channels (1950s = 2.9). Of those 35 channels, does anyone know how many the typical adult-viewer watches in any given week? 7.5.How many will you watch when there are 500 channels?*
- *The average household views over 7 hours a day/ 51 hours a week.*
- *VCR penetration is 83 percent. That's a lot of taping.*
- *But only half of all home-recorded tapes are ever played back.*
- *30 percent of all households have PCs.*

• *Advertising is still the lifeblood of television: in 1950, $171 million was spent on total TV advertising. Now it's at $33 billion!*

But beyond over-the-air broadcasting and cable, what are the alternate technologies being developed as means of delivering television?

There's DBS, direct broadcasting satellite. This system will beam a package of channels directly to homes that have small dish antennae. This service is scheduled to launch nationally this year. Another new competing delivery system is microwave technology. This simultaneously transmits dozens of channels for television, telephone, and data. Homes are reached by bouncing the signal off buildings or other objects until it reaches its destination.

But everything we've been discussing so far—the evolution of television, the new technologies—while dramatic and exciting, pales in comparison to the changes at hand.

A radically changed medium lies just around the corner, and the key to it is the coming electronic or information superhighway, which will use fiberoptic wires to compress and deliver 500, 600, or even 1,000 channels!

But will this lead to revolution— or total confusion?

Here's where the real opportunities lie. John Sculley, the former chief executive of Apple Computer, estimated that the formation of a single interactive information industry could generate revenue of $3.5 trillion by the year 2001.

The potential is enormous, but so is the massive outlay of capital required to finance this superhighway: over $400 billion (that's more than the gross national product of Canada). That's also why cable companies that until now have enjoyed virtual monopolies in their service areas are suddenly rushing into a series of mergers and partnerships with the one industry they most feared as future competition: the telephone companies. The Baby Bells are cash cows and they have the capital and resources to build and deliver the infrastructure to the information superhighway. Of course, a great deal of the direction and growth in this area is tied to government regulations. One of the greatest fears caused by all the recent megamergers is access, the ability of everyone—companies, consumers, institutions—to tap into the superhighway. Will a small number of "gatekeepers" be able to cause a "bottleneck"? How do Congress and the courts plan to enforce access?

There will be a lot of new words in our vocabulary—"multiplexing," "CD-ROM," "access"—that's the new language of the superhighway. Other buzzwords include fiber optics, infrastructure, signal compression, high definition, servers, interactive programming, multimedia, video dial tones, network time shifting, video on demand, bulletin board services, and virtual reality, with more and more coming on-line every day. But none of this is speculation. It isn't Buck Rogers fantasizing. It's what we are now capable of achieving.

What shape will the superhighway take? One senior cable executive offered this example: one of a 600-channel universe.

- *First, a 100-channel "grazing zone" that would be similar to current traditional cable television*
- *Next, there would be a 200-channel "quality zone" providing two additional channels for each channel in the "grazing zone" on which their best programming would be repeated*

- *Beyond that, a 50-channel "event TV zone" for live pay-per-view events such as boxing—and finally*
- *A 250-channel "video store" that would be reserved for movies, and these movies won't all necessarily be previously released theatricals; they may be big-budget spectaculars running concurrently with or prior to their theatrical runs*

What about programming on the superhighway? As a viewer, what would I find in the proposed grazing zone? Programming not meant as a mass viewing experience but designed for the individual: What I or you want, when we want it. For instance, movies that can now be ordered at several specific times during the day will be available at any time at all— virtually "on demand."

Incidentally, another example of "video on demand" is a system developed by a company called U.S.A. Video, which will digitize and compress full libraries of movie studios. Those compressed signals will be sent over telephone lines and stored in a box attached to a user's set, where they can keep the movie or event for up to 24 hours with the ability to rewind, fast forward, or pause it—just like a rented video.

But as a programmer, competing with hundreds of other channels, how will I effectively reach as many viewers as possible?

One of the strategies prominently mentioned by the broadcast networks and their cable counterparts is "multiplexing"—expanding their lineup to more than one channel at a time. For instance, it's Monday at 8 P.M. and HBO-One will be running a movie, while HBO-Two has a concert, and HBO-Three carries the series *Dream-On.*

What about the enormous potential of pay-per-view? Theatrical premieres and special events notwithstanding, the greatest example of a built-in pay-per-view audience is in sports. Thus far, only boxing, wrestling, and Howard Stern have managed to take full advantage of this technology; but the day of the pay-per-view "season ticket" will soon be at hand. It's speculated that the NFL could soon be offering a weekly tray of "pay-per-view" games if you want to watch a game other than the one carried in your market. And there will be special plans offered, if you wish to follow one particular out-of-town team for an entire season.

What about "interactive programming"? Forget the image of the couch potato who sits before his set going from channel to channel in a semivegetative state, the way my generation watches television. We're going to be replaced by a new generation of viewers raised on interacting with their sets. I can just hear an incredulous child saying to a parent, "You mean you used to watch movies without being able to decide what happens next?" Imagine reaching the last scene in *Casablanca* and then getting to choose who Ingrid Bergman goes off with at the end? Humphrey Bogart or Paul Heinreid? Heinreid wouldn't stand a chance!

But is this really what viewers want? To pick the end of their favorite television shows or films? Or does that somehow diminish the viewing experience? As a novelty, it might work, but on a regular basis?

At the recent superhighway summit at UCLA, opinion was split—Jeffrey Katzenberg, the chairman of the Walt Disney Studios, said that as a viewer he wouldn't want to sit home and determine the outcome of films. On the other hand, Lucie Salhany, the Fox Broadcasting Corporation chairman, says that this is something they are interested in and want to explore. Two major studios with opposite views.

Again, revolution or total confusion?

"Virtual reality," the sexiest of the new buzzwords, is another form of interactivity. The user is able to interact in what is usually a computer-driven environment. For example, batting against a major league pitcher while sitting in your living room. This experience is enhanced with video, audio, and graphics and gives the senses a full three-dimensional effect.

But "interactive programming" goes far beyond just playing simulated games or having your kids interact with *Beavis and Butthead*. By the way, that thought alone is enough to make me want to rethink the entire technology. But it's about interacting with other people. Interactive television will revolutionize education, politics, lifestyles.

Vice President Gore, the Clinton Administration's point man on the information superhighway, told CEOs at the UCLA summit that providing every school, library, and hospital with access to the superhighway's educational and informational tools was the highest priority and targeted the end of the decade for them to meet that challenge, which the CEOs in turn pledged to do.

Interactive television will change politics, careers, communication. Interest groups, scattered by geography, will be able to "link up," becoming much more effective, much more demanding. For those looking for a different quality of life, it will be much easier to run a business in a remote area, without leaving your home.

And you won't have to go out to do your marketing either. Instead of a trip to the supermarket, you'll be able to call up a market's entire inventory—by price, by brand, by size—and place your order by touching your screen. From foods, to fashion, to furnishing your home, to any aspect of your life—you'll soon be able to satisfy your shopping needs via video malls. In fact, *Joan Rivers Shopping Show* aside, the whole concept of home shopping has an enormous upside that has barely been scratched.

Also, let me mention briefly "high definition" television. It's important to realize that the quality of the images you'll be seeing on-screen, in the high-definition universe, will be taking a quantum leap. Not only will we have greater options regarding what to watch, but it will be provided in a widescreen format with unprecedented clarity. The audio will also be beyond anything previously available, and you'll be able to hang it all on your wall. Today's sets will seem as primitive and outmoded as the black-and-white sets of the fifties.

Yet, even with all the terms used to describe the future of the superhighway—enormous, gargantuan, unlimited—the bottom line is that no one agrees regarding what form it will finally take. With companies investing hundreds of millions, even billions of dollars, there's still no consensus on how it will pay off. Mistakes will be made. There won't be a magic switch that you turn on and it will suddenly be there.

Again, returning to my earlier analogy about Columbus setting sail for the New World: Where there are great opportunities, there are also great dangers. Will too much emphasis be placed on technologies and not enough on services being designed and how they impact people?

In fact, we can go down an entire list of questions posed by the advent of the superhighway:

- *How long will it take to construct? Five years or fifteen?*
- *How much will it cost?*

- *How much are consumers willing to pay for it?*
- *Will the superhighway mean the end of privacy? With everything one watches or orders being logged, where are the safeguards?*
- *What is the role of government?*
- *What is the future of over-the-air broadcasting?*
- *What kind of balance will be reached between interactive and passive programming?*
- *With so many specialized cable channels already here or on the horizon, are you ready for the cowboy channel and the mystery channel; the senior citizen, video game, talk show, and game show channels? What is the future of the mass-viewing experience?*
- *How will advertisers get their messages to viewers with itchy fingers on their remotes?*
- *What do television home shopping malls mean for local businesses?*
- *Will newspapers and magazines become obsolete?*
- *Is a computer-literate society necessarily a literate society?*
- *Will the superhighway create a generation able to cocoon itself by never leaving the house? Will interactive programming in a sense replace social interactivity?*

Obviously, if the future of television is a superhighway, we're only now approaching the onramp. We stand on the threshold of a convergence of technologies: cable, computers, VCRs, satellites, and fiber-optic networks.

The forthcoming explosion is the technological equivalent of the big bang, creating a new universe of almost limitless possibilities. We will be able to move information on a massive scale. For example, fax machines are currently capable of moving 14,000 bytes per second. By the turn of the century and with the new technology, it will be 1-billion bytes per second.

Well, for the last 30 minutes we covered just the headlines of what television was and what it will be. So, in closing, we ask the question again. Television in the nineties: is it revolution or confusion? Obviously from my remarks tonight, you know that I feel that the answer is: it's both.

In fact, your future home entertainment equipment will be so sophisticated that it's probably going to take either Einstein or a seven-year-old to work it.

I'll end by quoting one of the industry's giants and futurists, Ted Turner. He recently said, "Even with all these great technological breakthroughs and advances, most of my friends still can't program their VCRs and get the 12 to stop blinking."

Thank you.

AFTERWORD

Daniel E. Diamond

Dean, The Undergraduate College
New York University
Leonard N. Stern School of Business

The Stern School of Business is one of the oldest and most respected schools of business in this country and the world. Founded in 1900 by Charles Waldo Haskins as the School of Commerce, Accounts, and Finance, it pioneered in the development of professional accounting education at the collegiate level. Since virtually all of its enrollees were part-time students, it opened satellite programs in a number of locations in the New York City/ metropolitan area, including the Wall Street financial district. By World War I there were enough baccalaureate graduates who were interested in advanced work to initiate a graduate degree program. In 1916, the School of Commerce's Wall Street branch became the home of New York University's

Graduate School of Business Administration (GBA).

By the 1920s, the School of Commerce's programs were sufficiently broad to warrant the awarding of the Bachelor of Science degree. It was the first business school to do so. In the 1920s and 1930s, the School experienced continued growth in both the quality and breadth of its programs of study. The post–World War II period was one of unprecedented growth in the number of students at the School of Commerce and the Graduate School of Business Administration, as both veterans and high school graduates chose business school in record numbers.

In the 1960s, following the publication of the Ford and Carnegie Foundations' critical studies of collegiate business education, both Commerce and GBA fundamentally restructured their respective missions. Admissions and faculty hiring, promotion and tenure standards—all were raised. Henceforth, all business majors were built on a solid liberal arts base. Programs of study were refocused to stress conceptual and analytical material. Wherever possible they were related to the appropriate arts and science discipline.

In the 1970s, reflecting its new curriculum and

outlook, the School of Commerce was renamed the College of Business and Public Administration (BPA). At the same time, it moved to new, modern quarters in its present home—Tisch Hall. To strengthen its research and teaching, the faculty of BPA and GBA were merged into a joint Faculty of Business at New York University, simultaneously serving both undergraduate and graduate students.

In 1985, the Faculty of Business embarked on the formulation of a strategic, long-range plan. In 1987, it approved a major reorientation and restructuring of New York University's business schools. A year later, after receiving endorsements from the University's central administration and board of trustees, the plan was launched. At the same time, the University announced a $30 million gift to the business schools by Leonard N. Stern, an alumnus of both the School of Commerce and the Graduate School of Business Administration, as well as a trustee of the University. In recognition of Mr. Stern's extraordinary benefaction, the trustees renamed the business schools the Leonard N. Stern School of Business with an undergraduate college and a graduate division. Mr. Stern is the chairman and chief executive officer of The Hartz Group, Inc. His gift, thus far, is the largest single contribution to support collegiate business education in the United States.

The long-range plan is a comprehensive educational effort to create uncompromising academic excellence in all phases of the Stern School's activities. In so doing, it will enable the School's graduates to better meet the daunting demands of leadership for the balance of the 1990s and the 21st century beyond. Many of it major components have been implemented, including:

1. The consolidation of the faculty and the graduate and undergraduate divisions in a new, state-of-the-art, three-building Management Education Center at the University's main Washington Square Campus.
2. A 20-percent reduction in the student body at both the undergraduate and graduate levels with a concomitant improvement in the student/faculty ratio.
3. A refocusing of the MBA program to increase the relative importance of the full-time day program and to stabilize part-time enrollment at 2,000 students.
4. The development of new MBA and BS degrees curricula that strengthen the core curriculum by

requiring more work in management communications, business ethics and values, globalization and operations management; providing more holistic and integrated programs of study; offering increased opportunities for team and group work; and utilizing more applied business research.

5. A change in hiring, promotion, and tenure standards to bring teaching and education up to the same level of importance as research.

6. The adoption of a quality standard for the classroom presentation skills of the faculty.

7. The consolidation of the graduate division's library collections with the existing volumes at the University's main Bobst Library to create a world-class business research and reference library.

Presently, the Stern School's graduate division is consistently rated by both *Business Week* and *U.S. News & World Report* as one of the nation's top twenty business schools. For many years, its undergraduate college has been included in the top ten list by *The Gourman Report*. The long-range plan has the potential to further improve the Stern School rankings.

Despite the many changes envisioned by the plan, the Stern School will continue its many proud traditions. These include producing outstanding business leaders (Standard & Poor's biennial survey of the top executives at America's major corporations lists New York University's Stern School of Business as second only to Harvard in terms of where these individuals earned their degrees); being a school of opportunity at the undergraduate level for immigrants and the sons and daughters of immigrants; and serving as a forum for the discussion of the leading economic, financial, and management issues of the day, as evidenced by the lectures and conferences sponsored by the Joseph I. Lubin Memorial Lecture Series, the Center for Japan/U.S. Business and Economic Studies, and the NYU/Salomon Center for the Study of Financial Institutions.